PROFESSIONAL STUDIO TE

D0473005

DESIGN ESSENTIALS

Fourth Edition

Luanne Seymour Cohen

Design Essentials, Fourth Edition

by Luanne Seymour Cohen

Copyright © 2003 by Luanne Seymour Cohen

This Adobe Press book is published by Peachpit Press.

For information on Adobe Press books, contact:

Peachpit Press

1249 Eighth Street

Berkeley, CA 94710

510/524-2178 (tel) / 510/524-2221 (fax)

To report errors, please send a note to errata@peachpit.com.

Peachpit Press is a division of Pearson Education.

For the latest on Adobe Press books go to http://www.adobe.com/adobepress.

Editor: Becky Morgan

Production Coordinator: Kate Reber

Copyeditor: Judy Walthers von Alten

Indexer: Judy Walthers von Alten

Production Design: Jan Martí, Command Z

Cover design: Michael Mabry

ISBN 0-201-71363-2

9 8 7 6 5 4 3 2

Printed and bound in the United States of America

Acknowledgments

Writing a book is a lot like building a house. It takes a host of skilled people with diverse talents. Many people helped me with this book, and I would like to thank them. First, and foremost, I want to thank my family for their love and support. My husband **Rick**, my son **Charlie**, and my daughter **Jessica** help me keep perspective and curb my workaholic tendencies. **Judy Walthers von Alten**, as always, has been a wonderful and very professional editor. **Jan Martí** gets the award for production designer of the year: She weathered floods, sickness, and death but never gave up. My friends **Gay Allen**, **Joan Passarelli**, and **Debbie Ford** patiently listened to me discuss the ups and downs of writing during our daily hikes. **Kaoru Hollin** created some beautiful sample illustrations and, along with **Carol Bly**, tested the final manuscript. **Becky Morgan**, my Peachpit Press editor, listened to my gripes and gently prodded me to meet deadlines, always managing to stay cool, calm, and professional. **Russell Brown** and **Lisa Trail** helped keep me in touch with my readers by inviting me to ADIM in Monterey, California. **Michael Mabry** agreed to do the cover design on a short deadline with a small budget because he's a really nice guy—a really, really, nice guy. **Patricia Catanzaro** and **Dr. Johnny Wang** kept my repetitive strain injuries to a minimum. **Jill Merlin, Tanya Wendling,** and **Joan Delfino** at Adobe, and **Nancy Ruenzel** and **Kate Reber** of Peachpit Press also helped make this book possible. Thank you!

I'd also like to thank some of the people who didn't help me make this book, but who inspired my images. Thank you to my family, my parents, my siblings and their families, and my friends. Specifically, my mother, **Linda Bales**, who is a fabulous cook, inspired Bella Linda Foods. Richard's Pub is named for her husband, **Chic**. My daughter **Jessica** was the model for the Arabian nights illustration. My son **Charlie** and my other "daughter," **Chelsea Allen**, are the beachcombers. My brother **Doug Seymour** and his wife **Laura** own the Little Juice Shack in Hawaii. **Dean Read** *is* the CryoMan. My sister **Jill Seymour** and her partner **Shelly Tonge** are Seymour Tonge & Co. Their daughter **Emma** is EmmaGirl. I made the textured pattern quilt design for my brother **Brett Robinson**'s boat bed. I have a bad dog who lives at my house and his name is **Sam**. My husband's mother, **Basha Cohen**, pictured in the color-tinting technique, died of breast cancer in the early 1960s. **Rick**, my husband, is a fabulous rib-barbeque chef. My father, **Dale Seymour**, is a math educator and art lover. Our friends **Evan** and **Bruce Arnold** play in a garage band with my son and my husband; the band is called the Mama's Boys and the Papas. And finally, thank you to the Sea Hags for your inspiration and support—**Sue Arnold, Sarah Williams,** and **Leslie Cutler**. This Sea Hag is finished. Thank you all very much.

About the author

Luanne Seymour Cohen has been a graphic designer for the last 25 years. Some of the Silicon Valley companies she has worked for include Atari, Apple Computer, and Adobe Systems. She was a Creative Director at Adobe for 12 years where she created package designs and illustrations, and produced a variety of collateral materials for Adobe and its software products. She also developed and designed the Adobe Collector's Edition products. Her responsibilities included working closely with the engineers as an advisor during the development of Adobe's graphics software. She wrote and art-directed the first three editions of *Design Essentials* and another book in the series, *Imaging Essentials.* She has authored several books in the Classroom in a Book Series including *Adobe Illustrator 10 Classroom in a Book* and *Adobe Photoshop 6.0 and Adobe Illustrator 9.0 Advanced Classroom in a Book.* Some of her award-winning work has been shown in *Communication Arts, Print* magazine, the *Type Directors Club, Print* casebooks, and the AIGA annual. She has taught workshops and classes all over the world including at Stanford University, Kent State University, University of California at Santa Barbara, Anderson Ranch Arts Center, Center for Creative Imaging, the Thunder Lizard Photoshop and Illustrator conferences, and California College of Arts and Crafts. An avid quilter for more than 35 years, she has taught classes and written articles on digital quilt and fabric design. In 1995, she published a book, *Quilt Design Masters,* with Dale Seymour Publications/Addison Wesley. The book is used in elementary school classrooms to teach mathematical principles. She lives and works in the San Francisco Bay Area, where she teaches art at Springer Elementary School.

Contents

Introduction

Design Essentials, Fourth Edition shows how to produce traditional graphic and photographic effects using Adobe Photoshop and Adobe Illustrator software. This book, like the other books in the Professional Studio Techniques series, does not attempt to describe the features of these software programs. Instead, it is a quick, how-to recipe book for artists familiar with the basic tools and commands in the programs.

Because the software has changed so much between the publication of *Design Essentials, Third Edition* and now, all of the techniques are new or have been completely rewritten. Each technique has been tested extensively by professional designers, Web page designers, illustrators, teachers, photographers, and novice users. Even though I make the assumption that the reader has a fundamental working knowledge of the software, I have included an appendix that reviews the fundamental shortcuts and commands that I use every day with these programs. I've also included a recommended reading list. You can find an overwhelming number of Photoshop and Illustrator books to help you learn more about these very versatile programs. My list includes only books that I think offer accurate, well-researched, and well-designed information.

Design Essentials, Fourth Edition covers the most recent versions of the Adobe software for both Macintosh and Windows platforms: Adobe Photoshop 7.0 and Adobe Illustrator 10. Many, but not all, of these techniques can be used with older versions of the software. The required software for each technique is indicated beneath the technique title. Look for the shortcuts in the appendix. When keys are indicated in the text, I use a slash (/) to separate the Macintosh and Windows key needed. For example:

> "Press the Option/Alt key when clicking on a button" means
> **Macintosh** users press the Option key.
> **Windows** users press the Alt key.

—Luanne Seymour Cohen

1 Painting

Painted paper illustrations

Adobe Photoshop 7.0
Adobe Illustrator 10 or later (optional)

Some illustrators use a method of collage that requires making many sheets of painted paper. The paper is then cut into shapes that are combined to form the illustration. You can create your own digitally painted collage with this technique. Create your illustration outlines in Illustrator or use Photoshop to create the paths. Then make several layers of painted paper. For each paper layer, you'll add a layer mask to mask out the collage shapes. If you want a three-dimensional look, try adding a tiny drop shadow to the shapes. This technique works well with marbled paper (see the technique on page 116) as well. Just substitute the painted layer with a marbled layer.

1. Open a new RGB file in Photoshop. Create a new layer and name it Paint 1.

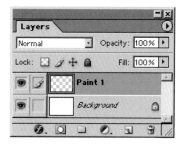

2. Select the brush tool in the toolbox. Choose Window > Brushes to display the Brushes palette. From the Brushes palette menu, choose Thick Heavy Brushes. When you get the warning dialog box, click Append to add the brushes to the existing list.

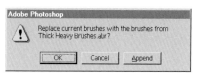

3. Scroll to the bottom of the list in the Brushes palette, and select the Flat Bristle brush. Depending on your file size, you may want to adjust the size of the brush. If so, increase or decrease the Master Diameter of the brush now.

4. Choose a foreground color, and set the tool's mode to Hard Light in the tool options bar.

5. Begin to paint the entire layer with the textured brush. Overlap the brush strokes for additional color and texture changes. Use the brush at different sizes and modes.

Set the brush to Multiply, Difference, or Vivid Light for different effects.

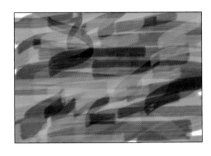

6. Create a new layer and name it Paint 2. Hide the Paint 1 layer.

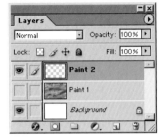

7. Repeat steps 3 through 6 for as many colors as you need for your illustration. Try using some of the other brushes for different textures. Try painting two or three similiar colors on the same layer.

8. If you are not copying the illustration paths from Illustrator, make an illustration with paths in Photoshop, and skip to step 11. If you are copying paths from Illustrator, open the illustration file in Illustrator. Choose Illustrator > Preferences > Files & Clipboard (OS X) or Edit > Preferences > Files & Clipboard. Select the AICB option, and choose Preserve Paths. Click OK.

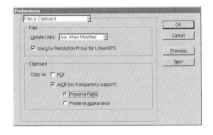

9. In Illustrator, select the illustration paths, and choose Edit > Copy.

10. Switch back to Photoshop, and choose Edit > Paste. In the dialog box that appears, select Path, and click OK.

Note: If you want to adjust the size of the paths before you make them into masks, select the paths with the Path selection tool. Then choose Edit > Free Transform Path to scale the path. Press Return/Enter to complete the transformation.

11. In the Paths palette, click the Work Path if it's not already selected. Choose the path selection tool and click one of the paths. Click the Load Path as Selection button at the bottom of the Paths palette.

12. Click in the blank area of the Paths palette to hide the paths from view. In the Layers palette, click the layer that you'll fill with the selection. Make sure that the layer is not hidden, and click the Add Layer Mask button.

13. If you want to rotate or scale the texture, unlink the mask from its layer. Click the layer thumbnail, and move, scale, or rotate the layer image. Using the Edit > Free Transform command, make the transformations needed, and press Return/Enter.

14. Repeat steps 11 through 13 for each of the paint layers that you made. Remember, you can select multiple objects and put them on one layer mask. In this example, the faces and hands are all on one layer mask.

Tissue-paper mosaics

Adobe Illustrator 10 or later

Using a rasterized image, you can create tiles that can be overlapped for a tissue-paper collage look or that can be organized with "grout" for a mosaic effect. Start with an illustration or a placed raster image, and begin experimenting. Leave the original artwork on a layer in the background, to fill in the holes that are left when transforming the tile artwork. You can also remove that layer for a confetti effect. For a stained glass effect, use black grout. Use images with big, bold shapes that are recognizable. Small details will be simplified and lost.

1. Create or open an illustration. If the artwork exists on several layers, choose Flatten Artwork from the Layers palette menu to reduce the file to one layer.

If you want to retain the file with separate layers, choose File > Save As, and save the flattened file with a different name.

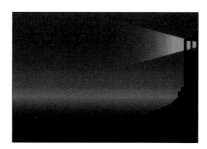

2. Drag the flattened layer onto the New Layer button at the bottom of the Layers palette to make a duplicate layer. Double-click the duplicate to open the Layer Options dialog box, and name it Tissue Paper. Lock the original layer.

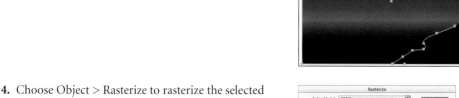

3. Choose Select > All.

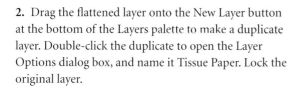

4. Choose Object > Rasterize to rasterize the selected image. Set the Anti-Aliasing option to Art Optimized (Supersampling). Select either Medium or Screen resolution. Click OK.

Because you will change this image to a mosaic of shapes, you don't need a high-resolution raster image.

5. With the selection still active, choose Filter > Create > Object Mosaic to turn the raster image into a mosaic of squares. Select the Delete Raster option, and enter the number of tiles you want for the Width. Click the Use Ratio button to have the height calculated and entered for you. Click OK.

6. Choose Object > Ungroup to release the mosaic tiles from their group. Choose View > Hide Edges so that the object remains selected and you can see the effect you will create in the next step.

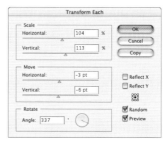

7. Choose Object > Transform > Transform Each to alter the tiles individually. Turn on the Preview option and increase the Scale values so that the tiles overlap. Turn on the Random option and change the Move and Rotate values for a less regular effect. When you are satisfied with the preview, click OK.

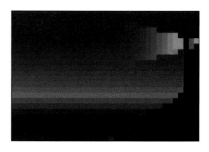

8. Choose View > Show Edges and then Select > Deselect to view the results.

9. Lock the Tissue Paper layer in the Layers palette and unlock the original layer.

10. Select different shapes on the original layer and alter their color slightly to set off the squares on the Tissue Paper layer. Save the file.

In this example, the colors in the background gradient were changed slightly. The light beam was made less transparent, and the rock and lighthouse were lightened.

Variation: Follow the first technique, except use larger scale values in step 7. After step 7, with the tiles still selected, choose Object > Ungroup. Target the Tissue Paper layer and then choose Effect > Pathfinder > Soft Mix. Leave the Mixing rate at 50% and click OK.

The Soft Mix simulates transparency where the tiles overlap. In this example, only the Tissue Paper layer is showing.

Tiles with grout

1. Follow steps 1 through 6 of the technique. Create a new layer and name it Grout. Move it just below the Tissue Paper layer. Create a rectangle the same size as the raster image rectangle, and fill it with a color that will appear between the tiles in the next step. Lock the Grout layer.

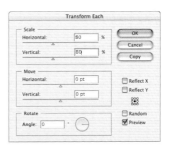

2. Continue with step 7, and reduce only the Horizontal and Vertical Scale percentages until you can see the Grout layer showing through the Tissue Paper layer. For an even thickness of grout, use the same value for both Horizontal and Vertical Scale. Click OK.

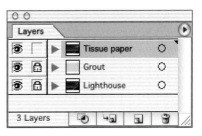

3. Save the file.

Because the grout is on a separate layer, you can easily select it and try as many different colors as you like.

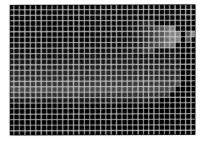

Painterly images

Adobe Photoshop 7.0 or later

Here's a way to turn your photographs into beautiful, textural digital paintings. Photoshop has many built-in filters that produce a painterly or sketchy texture. You'll separate the color from the texture to give you more control over the final effect. Several variations on the basic steps appear at the end of the technique. Just substitute the filter shown in the variation for the one used in step 8, and you'll get a very different result.

1. Open an RGB image. Much of the detail will be lost in this technique, so pick an image with a strong composition and vibrant colors.

The image should start in RGB mode because many of the filters used in this technique work only on RGB images.

2. Option/Alt-drag the Background layer thumbnail in the Layers palette onto the New Layer button to duplicate the background. Name this layer Texture. This layer will define only the texture of the final image, not the color.

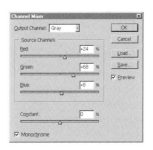

3. Choose Image > Adjustments > Channel Mixer. Select the Monochrome option to remove the color, and start out with the values in the example. Adjust for your image if necessary.

Using Channel Mixer has more flexibility than the Desaturate command.

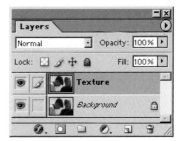

4. Duplicate the Background layer and name it Color. This layer will define the colors of your painting. Drag the Color layer above the Texture layer in the Layers palette.

5. Set the blending mode for the Color layer to Color. Then hide the Background and Texture layers.

The Color mode retains the color from that layer but picks up any texture from the layers beneath it.

6. With the Color layer still selected, choose Filter > Blur > Smart Blur. Experiment with the Radius and Threshold values until the image has a cartoony or airbrushed look. Set the Quality to High, and click OK.

Notice that the face details have been blurred away. Don't worry about the loss of details; they will be restored in the next step.

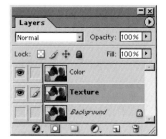

7. Select the Texture layer to make it active and visible.

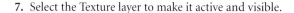

8. Choose Filter > Artistic > Dry Brush. You will get different texture effects depending on the resolution of your image. Experiment with different values until you are satisfied with the texture. Click OK.

This example of a 300-ppi image used a Brush Size of 3, a Brush Detail of 10, and a Texture of 2.

9. If you are satisfied with the effect, save or print the image. To experiment with other textures and effects, try the following variations.

Texturizer variation

Follow step 1 and then steps 4 through 6; don't create a texture layer. Choose Filter > Texture > Texturizer.

Settings:
Texture = Canvas
Scaling = 109%
Relief = 5
Light Dir. = Top Left

Colored Pencil variation

Press the D key to set the foreground and background colors to their defaults. Replace step 8 with: Choose Filter > Artistic > Colored Pencil.

Settings:
Pencil Width = 4
Stroke Pressure = 12
Paper Brightness = 25

Spatter variation
Replace step 8 with:
Choose Filter >
Brush Strokes >
Spatter.

Settings:
Spray Radius = 17
Smoothness = 5

Poster Edges variation
Replace step 8 with:
Choose Filter > Artistic >
Poster Edges.

Settings:
Edge Thickness = 1
Edge Intensity = 1
Posterization = 2

Rough Pastels variation
Replace step 8 with:
Choose Filter > Artistic >
Rough Pastels. Set the
Texture layer to 60%
opacity.

Settings:
Stroke Length = 12
Stroke Detail = 18
Texture = Canvas
Scaling = 50%
Relief = 29
Light Dir. = Left

**Sprayed Strokes
variation**
Replace step 8 with:
choose Filter >
Brush Strokes >
Sprayed Strokes.

Settings:
Stroke Length = 20
Spray Radius = 22
Stroke Direction =
  Left Diagonal

Cutout variation
Replace step 8 with:
Choose Filter > Artistic > Cutout.

Settings:
No. of Levels = 5
Edge Simplicity = 6
Edge Fidelity = 1

Watercolor variation
Replace step 8 with:
Choose Filter > Artistic > Watercolor.

Settings:
Brush Detail = 14
Shadow Intensity = 0
Texture = 1

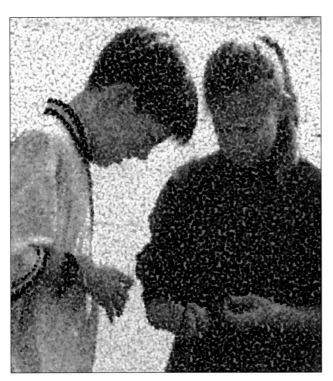

Pointillize variation
Replace step 8 with:
Set background color to 50% gray. Choose Filter > Pixelate > Pointillize.

Settings:
Cell Size = 5

Fresco variation
Replace step 8 with:
Set the texture layer to 75% opacity and choose Filter > Artistic > Fresco.

Settings:
Brush Size = 2
Brush Detail = 8
Texture = 1

Digital paintings

Adobe Photoshop 7.0 or later

In just a few simple steps, you can turn a run-of-the-mill snapshot or stock photo into a digital painting. Use the brushes available to you in the Photoshop Brushes palette, or create your own to add texture and a more painterly feel. You'll add texture by creating a canvas or paper texture layer. Then you'll create a pattern out of the image and use the pattern stamp tool to create an impressionistic painting from the original photo.

1. Open a new file. If the file has several layers, flatten them and choose File > Save As to save the file with a new name.

2. If your image has flat or dull colors, intensify them for the painting as needed. Create an adjustment layer by clicking the New Adjustment Layer button at the bottom of the Layers palette. Choose Hue/Saturation. Move the Saturation slider to the right to intensify the colors in your image. Click OK.

3. Choose Merge Down from the Layers palette menu to combine the adjustment layer with the image layer. Choose Window > History, and click the New Snapshot button to create a new snapshot of the current state of your image.

It's a good idea to take several snapshots as you make a painting. Snapshots let you go back to a stage that you liked, if needed.

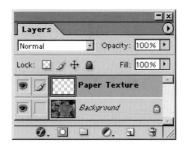

4. Create a new layer in the Layers palette, and name it Paper Texture (or Canvas Texture) depending on the texture you want to use.

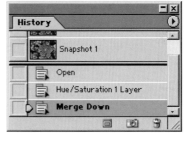

5. Choose Edit > Fill and fill the Paper or Canvas texture layer with White.

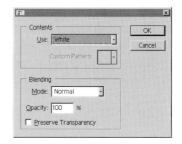

6. Choose Filter > Texture > Texturizer. Choose the Canvas texture, or select Load Texture from the Texture menu, navigate to Adobe Photoshop 7.0 > Presets > Textures, select the Stucco 2.psd file, and click Open.

Use the example settings or change them to suit your artwork. Look for more textures on your Photoshop CD in the Goodies > Textures for Lighting Effects folder.

7. Set the Paper Texture layer blending mode to Multiply. This lets you to see the image through the Paper Texture layer.

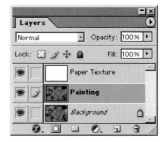

8. Click the Background layer in the Layers palette, and Option/Alt-drag it onto the New Layer button at the bottom of the palette to duplicate and name it. Name the new layer Painting.

9. Choose Select > All, and then Edit > Define Pattern to create a new pattern tile of the entire image. Name the pattern and click OK.

This pattern will be the image you'll use as the source for your painting.

10. With the Painting layer still selected, press Delete/Backspace to remove the image from that layer. Choose Select > Deselect.

The layer won't look different because you can still see the Background layer, but you'll see the difference in the Layers palette.

11. Select the pattern stamp tool in the toolbox. Turn on the Impressionist option in the options bar. Click the Pattern picker and select the pattern you created in step 9.

12. Select a brush in the Brushes palette, or create a custom brush that matches the texture of the subject matter.

Begin painting the image. The impressionist tool samples the colors that are in the snapshot and lets you move them around. Zoom in to paint certain sections or objects in your image.

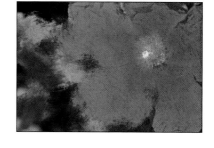

13. Continue to paint in the image on the Painting layer. If you want to see the image without the Background layer showing through, turn off the Background layer in the Layers palette.

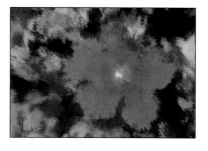

14. As you paint, change the brush size or brush stroke direction based on the subject matter. Continue painting until the image is complete. You can leave the Background layer turned on or off, according to your taste.

Painting foliage

Adobe Photoshop 7.0 or later

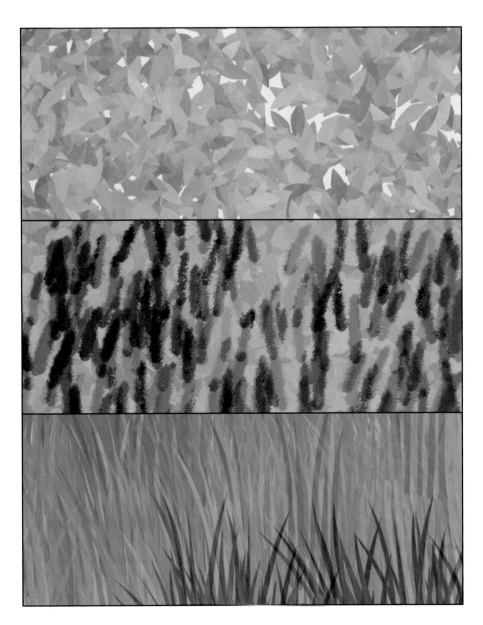

The Photoshop Brushes palette offers so many options, it is the perfect tool for creating brushes that can paint leaves, grass, flowers, and fields of grain. You can make an endless number of brushes to paint foliage. In this technique you'll create a leaf shape and define it as a brush. Then you'll customize it so that when you paint with it, you get a stream of randomly placed, rotated, scaled, and colored leaves—just as in nature. Try using several brushes on one tree or bush. If you want striped leaves, add a subtle, dark-gray stripe to the black leaf before you define it as a brush.

1. Open a new file in Photoshop. Press the D key to return the foreground and background colors to the defaults. Select the pen tool in the toolbox. Select the Shape Layers option in the tool options bar.

2. Draw a leaf shape. (This technique shows drawing a leaf, but you can use these instructions for grass or flowers as well.)

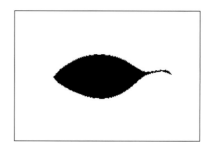

3. Choose Layer > Rasterize > Shape to change the vector shape into a raster shape. Double-click the Shape layer name, and change its name to Leaf Shape.

It's necessary to rasterize the shape because brushes can only be created from raster shapes or images. You will define the brush in the next step.

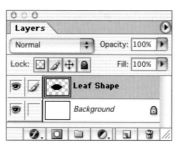

4. With the Leaf Shape layer still selected in the Layers palette, choose Edit > Define Brush. Name the brush Leaf 1, and click OK in the Brush Name dialog box.

5. Select the brush tool in the toolbox. Choose Window > Brushes to display the Brushes palette. Click Brush Tip Shape on the left side of the palette, scroll through the list, and click the Leaf 1 brush. If desired, adjust the diameter.

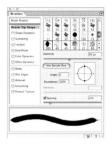

In this example, the diameter was reduced to 90 pixels from 385 pixels.

6. Click the name Shape Dynamics in the list on the left side of the Brushes palette. Clicking the words automatically selects the option and displays the controls for Shape Dynamics. Adjust the Size Jitter and the Angle Jitter using the preview at the bottom of the palette.

7. Click the name Scattering in the list on the left side of the Brushes palette. Adjust the Scatter, Count, and Count Jitter (randomness).

8. Click the name Color Dynamics in the list on the left side of the Brushes palette. Adjust the Hue Jitter.

You won't be able to preview the hue change until you actually paint—so guess. Hue Jitter specifies how much the foreground color will vary in hue with each brush stroke.

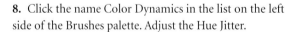

9. Click the New Brush button at the bottom of the Brushes palette. Name this brush Leaf 2.

Because you changed the dynamics and options of the Leaf 1 brush, you must save it as a new brush. Each time you change an option on a custom brush, you need to resave it.

10. Create a new layer, and name it Brush Test. Turn off the Leaf Shape layer.

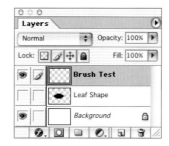

11. Select a foreground color that will be the basic leaf hue.

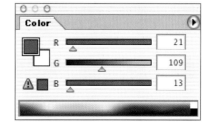

12. Use the brush tool to paint a few strokes on the Brush Test layer to test your brush. Evaluate the color, size, scatter amount, and number of leaves; then decide what you want to change.

You may want to change the brush settings in the tool options bar, too. For example, setting the blending mode to Color or Multiply produces a transparent, overlapping effect.

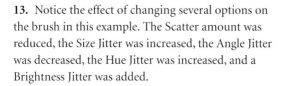

13. Notice the effect of changing several options on the brush in this example. The Scatter amount was reduced, the Size Jitter was increased, the Angle Jitter was decreased, the Hue Jitter was increased, and a Brightness Jitter was added.

14. Once you've created several brushes that you want to use again, save them as a brush library. Choose Save Brushes from the Brushes palette menu. Save them in the Presets/Brushes folder, inside the Photoshop program folder; the library name will appear alphabetically in the Brushes palette menu after you restart Photoshop.

Color-tinted photographs

Adobe Photoshop 7.0 or later

In traditional photography, photographers rely on post-darkroom techniques to enhance black-and-white prints with color. Sepia-toning and iron-toning are two of these techniques; these processes tone the overall print with brown and blue, respectively. Hand-coloring with oil paints is another technique traditionally used to add color to photographs—sometimes to make a print look more realistic and sometimes to create an artistic effect.

Color-tinting

1. Open the grayscale file you want to color-tint. Convert the file to RGB. If you are starting with a color image, choose Image > Adjustments > Desaturate to remove the existing color.

2. If the image is dark, click the New Adjustment Layer button at the bottom of the Layers palette and select Levels to create a new adjustment layer. Move the histogram highlight and midtone sliders to the left.

The goal here is to lighten the image so that you can clearly see the color-tinting.

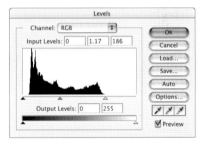

3. Select the area or shape to tint.

This selection has a feather value of 1 because the lips are not hard-edged.

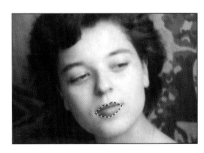

4. Option/Alt-click the New Fill Layer button at the bottom of the Layers palette to create a new Solid color layer. Set its mode to Color. Click OK.

By setting the blending mode now, you'll be able to see the results while choosing the color in step 5. The Color blending mode allows the layer's colors to overlay the value and texture of the grayscale image beneath it.

5. When the Color Picker appears, choose a color for your fill layer. If needed, move the Color Picker away from your image so that you can see the colors preview as you sample them.

Notice that the selection is no longer active but has become a layer mask for the fill layer.

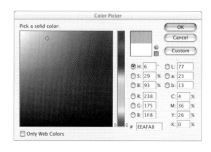

6. Once you are satisfied with the color effect, click OK.

The good thing about tinting with Fill layers is that you can always change the fill color later. To change the fill color, simply double-click the color thumbnail in the Layers palette to display the Color Picker. Change the color and click OK.

7. Repeat steps 3 through 6 for each area that needs tinting.

8. Create a new layer and set the blending mode to Multiply. Use a paintbrush or airbrush to add color to areas that are too light or that don't have much original texture.

In this example, more color was added to the right cheek to better match the left cheek.

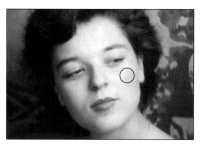

9. As a final step, double-click the Levels adjustment layer that you created in step 2. Move the Levels dialog box so that you can see the image and readjust the contrast level until you are satisfied with the result.

Sepia- and iron-toning

1. To make a sepia-tone photograph, follow the preceding steps 1 and 2. Choose Merge Visible from the Layers palette menu. Then choose Image > Adjustments > Variations.

Clicking the variations will gradually change the overall color of the image.

2. Set the slider two notches above Fine, and add Red and Yellow a couple of times. Then add Blue once to get a sepia tone.

To simulate iron-toning, follow these steps, but click the Blue, Cyan, and Green variations.

Selective color recovery

1. Open an RGB file and create a snapshot in the History palette. Follow steps 1 and 2 of the color-tinting procedure.

2. Make a new snapshot of the grayscale version. Set the source for the history brush to the color snapshot you took in step 1.

3. Create a new layer, select the history brush, and paint in the areas that you want to return to full color.

Or if you prefer, make selections and choose Edit > Fill. In the dialog box, choose History in the Contents pop-up menu and click OK. If you make an error or paint in too much color, set the history brush source to the grayscale snapshot, and repair the image.

Outlined images

Adobe Photoshop 7.0 or later

You can turn a flat or dull photograph into a graphic illustration with this technique. Start with an image that has edges that you want to emphasize. The best images for this technique are simple without a lot of contrasty texture. You'll end up with a Color layer that has a softened, airbrushed look to it, and with an Outline layer that overlays the Color layer. There are a couple of variations on the types of outlines you can make. Try each of them with your image to see which looks best.

1. Open an image that you want to outline. Use an image of at least 300 dpi because the outline edges look better. Images that have interesting, clearly defined edges work best.

2. Option/Alt-drag the layer you want to outline to the New Layer button at the bottom of the Layers palette to duplicate the layer. Name the layer Color.

This example shows the Background layer duplicated.

3. To intensify the colors, create an adjustment layer by clicking the New Adjustment Layer button at the bottom of the Layers palette and selecting Hue/ Saturation.

You'll make the image look more like an illustration by creating a more surreal color scheme.

4. Adjust the Hue, Saturation, or Lightness to make your image more dramatic.

Each image will require a different adjustment. You can change an adjustment layer at any time, so you'll be able to make more color changes later if needed.

5. Select the Color layer, and choose Filter > Blur > Smart Blur. Set the Quality to High and the Mode to Normal. Start with the Radius and Threshold values shown here, and then adjust them for your image. The goal is to smooth out the inside of the shapes while retaining crisp edges. Click OK.

6. Evaluate the resulting Color layer. It should be missing much of its original texture. The shapes should be simplified and have well-defined edges. If you are not satisfied with the result, undo, and try step 5 again with different values.

7. Option/Alt-drag the Color layer to the New Layer button at the bottom of the Layers palette to duplicate the layer. Name this layer Outline.

8. Choose Image > Adjustments > Channel Mixer to remove the color from the image. Select Monochrome and use these settings: R = 24, G = 68, B = 8. Adjust the values if necessary to retain the edge detail in your image. Click OK.

Removing the color before you create the outlines gives you the black edges in step 9.

9. Create the outlines by choosing Filter > Stylize > Find Edges.

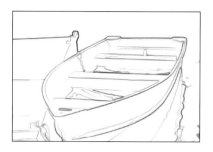

10. Set the Outline layer mode to Darken. If you are satisfied with the result, stop here. If the image still needs some finessing, continue with step 11.

Darken applies only the dark edges to the image. The white areas are ignored.

11. If the outlines are too weak or too thick, correct them with another adjustment layer. Option/Alt-click the New Adjustment Layer button and select Brightness/Contrast. Select the Group With Previous Layer option. Click OK.

12. Adjust the Brightness/Contrast values until you are satisfied with the outlines. Click OK.

To make the lines darker, reduce the brightness and increase the contrast. To make the lines lighter, increase the brightness and decrease the contrast.

Variation 1: If you want less black and more color in your outlines, skip step 8. Then set the Outline layer mode to Multiply.

Variation 2: If you want a bitmap-quality outline, use the Smart Blur filter instead of the Find Edges filter in step 9. Choose Filter > Blur > Smart Blur, and use the Edge Only mode. Then choose Image > Adjustments > Invert to invert the Outline layer, and continue with step 10.

Neon graphics

Adobe Photoshop 7 or later
OR Adobe Illustrator 10 or later

Making graphics glow in Photoshop and Illustrator is easy, but making digital neon is a different matter. Real neon signs and graphics are made from colored tubes filled with gas. The tubes are the same width and are wrapped and twisted to make shapes and letterforms. To make digital neon, use paths created in either Illustrator or Photoshop. Then create a tubal gradation by layering progressively smaller stroked paths on top of each other. Following are directions for making neon in both Photoshop and Illustrator. They both take about the same number of steps, but the Illustrator method (starting on page 40) is more versatile because you can save the appearance as a style, edit it, and reuse it without re-creating the neon each time.

Photoshop method

1. Design the neon base artwork using the pen tool in either Photoshop or Illustrator. Leave plenty of space between the paths so that you can increase the line thickness.

2. Create a background in Photoshop that is black or contains very dark tones to set off the neon artwork. Make a new layer and call it Neon 1.

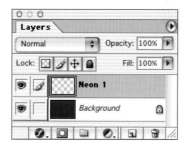

3. If you created your paths in Photoshop, skip to step 5. If you created your artwork in Illustrator, check the paste preferences before you copy the artwork. Choose Illustrator > Preferences > Files & Clipboard (OS X) or Edit > Preferences > Files & Clipboard (Mac OS and Windows). Select the Copy As AICB option and choose Preserve Paths.

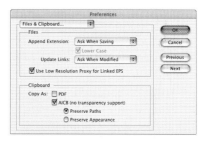

4. Copy the paths and paste them into your Photoshop file. Select the Paste As Path option. Click OK.

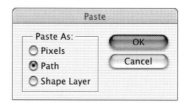

5. Double-click the Work Path name in the Paths palette and save the path.

Note: All paths can be on the same pathname.

6. Select the first path or paths that share the same color.

You can press the Command/Ctrl key when any tool is selected, and the pointer will change to the arrow tool when the pointer is positioned over a path.

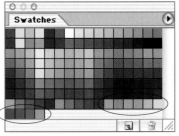

7. Create a set of three or four colors for the neon glow. You'll want a bright glow color and one or two midtone colors. Add them to your Swatches palette for later use.

This example used a green set of three (body), a yellow set of three (hair), and a red set of four (skateboard) colors.

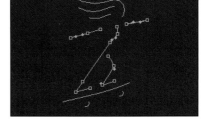

8. Select the brush tool in the toolbox. Set the mode to Normal and the Flow to 50% in the tool options bar.

9. Click the arrow next to the brush sample to reveal the Brushes palette. Select a large soft-edged brush.

This will be the width of the outer glow of the neon tube. All the other brushes used will be smaller than this one.

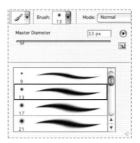

10. Choose the Neon layer and select the second brightest color from the swatches you saved in step 7. With the path or paths still selected, choose Stroke Subpaths from the Paths palette menu. It will show you that the brush is the selected tool. Click OK.

A shortcut for stroking an active path with the current tool is to press Return/Enter.

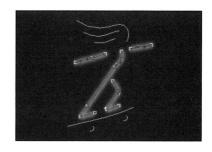

11. Choose a smaller soft brush. Select one of the midtone colors from the swatches you created.

If you want the flexibility to adjust the colors later, make a different layer for each new stroke color. To change the colors easily, lock the transparent pixels for those layers before you fill with a new color.

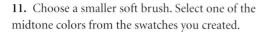
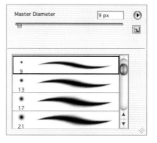

12. Stroke the path with the new color and brush the same way you did in step 10.

13. Select a smaller brush than you did in step 10. Select the brightest color in your swatch set.

For a more defined tube highlight, choose a much smaller brush than the last one used. If you want a softer gradation of color, reduce it by one brush size.

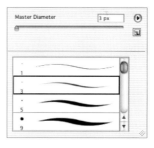

14. Stroke the path with the new color and brush the same way you did in step 9. Deselect the paths for a better preview.

15. Repeat steps 9 through 14 for each different color path or paths.

In this example, four different colors and brushes were used for the red skateboard.

Illustrator method

1. Create a Background layer that is black or contains very dark tones to set off the neon artwork. Lock the Background layer. Make a new layer and call it Neon.

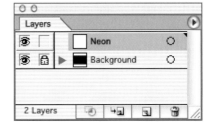

2. On the Neon layer, create the neon artwork using the pen tool or a shape creation tool (e.g., star, rectangle, and so on). Leave plenty of space between the paths so that you can increase the line thickness.

3. Choose Show Options from the Stroke palette menu. Select the Round Cap and Round Join options.

These options make the stroked paths look more like curved tubes.

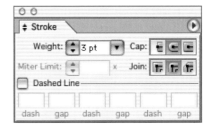

4. With the path or paths still selected, choose a fill of None and a stroke of None.

The neon paint colors will be added as an appearance for the Neon layer. If individual paths are already painted, their paint can change or obscure the look of the neon style.

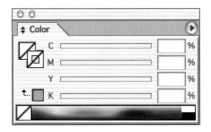

5. In the Layers palette, click the target indicator for the Neon layer. Targeting a layer lets you affect the entire layer when you add an appearance.

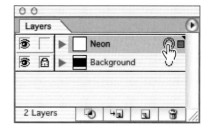

6. From the Appearance palette menu, choose Add New Stroke.

A stroke is added with the default color and width. You will change these in the next steps.

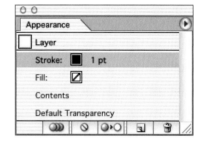

7. Select the stroke weight and choose the Round Cap and Round Join options. This stroke will be the base color and the widest stroke of the neon tube.

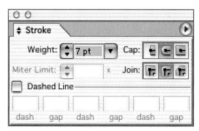

8. In the Color palette, change the stroke color to the base color of the neon. This will be the darkest part of the neon tube.

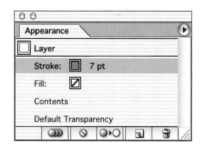

9. With the stroke still selected in the Appearance palette, choose Effect > Blur > Gaussian Blur. Set the radius and click OK.

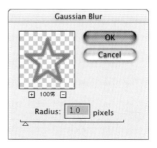

10. Evaluate the base level of the neon. You may want to change the resolution of the Gaussian Blur effect if it appears too blurred or too jagged. The default resolution for these effects is 72 ppi. If you want to change it, continue with step 11. If not, go to step 12.

11. To change the raster settings for the Gaussian Blur effect, choose Effect > Document Raster Effects Settings. Select the resolution desired and click OK.

The higher the resolution, the longer it will take for your graphics to preview.

12. Make sure that the Neon layer is still targeted. Select the stroke in the Appearance palette, and choose Duplicate Item from the palette menu.

13. Reduce the stroke weight and change the color to a lighter version of the base color. Double-click the Gaussian Blur item to reopen the Gaussian Blur dialog box. Reduce the amount of blur.

In this example, the Gaussian blur amount was reduced by half to match the stroke weight reduced by nearly half.

14. Repeat steps 12 and 13 to create one last stroke. This one will represent the brightest, hottest part of the neon effect. Make the color bright and much lighter than the other two. Reduce the stroke weight and Gaussian blur as well.

15. Evaluate the effect. Depending on the resolution you chose in step 11, the stroke weight and blur amount will vary. The higher the resolution, the higher the blur amount will need to be for a smooth, rounded effect. If you need to adjust colors, stroke weights, or blur amounts, just double-click them in the Appearance palette and change the values.

Saving the neon effect as a style

1. Position the Appearance palette and the Styles palette so that they are both visible. Drag the thumbnail of the appearance from the Appearance palette onto the Styles palette until the thick, black border appears. Release the mouse button to create a style. If you want to name it, double-click the thumbnail in the Styles palette and enter a name.

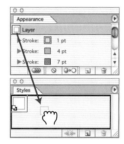

2. Now that you have created a style, it can be applied to layers or individual paths. You can also change the colors or stroke weights to create a new style.

In this example, the neon style was applied to the rectangle and then the colors for each stroke were changed. The resolution was set to Medium (150 ppi).

Cast shadows

Adobe Photoshop 7.0 or later

One of the toughest types of images to make is a really good composite. A few tricks, however, help create the illusion that different images from different photos fit together. One trick is to make realistic cast shadows. This technique takes you through the basic steps of how to place an object into a background, adjust its color, and create a cast shadow. You may need to deviate from the instructions for your images. Try different colors for the shadow, or play with different transformation amounts in step 8. If you don't get the gradation angle correct in step 13, keep trying until you're happy with it.

1. Open an RGB image that will be the background for your composite image.

Notice the color of the light and the direction of the shadows.

2. Open another file and select the object you want to bring into the background image.

Pay attention to the light color and shadow direction. In this example, the light is coming from the opposite direction and is much cooler than in the background image. These problems will be corrected later.

3. Use the move tool to drag the object onto the background. A new layer will be created. Select Layer Properties from the Layers palette menu and name this layer Object. Position the object, and scale and flip the image if necessary. Notice that the elephant seems to float in the air without a cast shadow.

4. Option/Alt-drag the Object layer thumbnail onto the New Layer button to create a duplicate. Name this layer Shadow. Select the Lock Transparent Pixels option for the Shadow layer.

5. Use the eyedropper tool to select a shadow color from the shadows in the background image. If no shadows exist, create a dark color in the Color palette.

6. Fill the Shadow layer with the foreground color.

Because the transparent pixels are locked, only the areas on the layer that contain pixels are filled.

7. Move the Shadow layer down in the Layers palette so that it is below the Object layer. Turn off the Lock Transparent Pixels option for the Shadow layer.

8. With the Shadow layer still selected, choose Edit > Transform > Distort. Grab one corner of the shadow to pull it in the direction you want it to fall. Continue to transform the shadow until its shape and angle match the light angle and direction. Make sure that the base of the shadow touches the object that casts the shadow. Press Return/Enter to complete the transformation.

9. Choose Filter > Blur > Gaussian Blur. Turn on the Preview option so that you can decide which Radius amount works for your image. When it looks right, click OK.

The Radius amount depends on resolution and existing shadows. Try to match the edge softness of other shadows in the background.

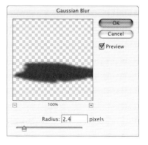

10. Set the Shadow layer blending mode to Multiply and adjust the Opacity.

The Multiply mode darkens the layers underneath but still allows the texture of the lower layers to show through.

11. Select the Object layer in the Layers palette. Option/Alt-click the New Adjustment Layer button and drag to choose either Levels or Curves from the pop-up menu. Select the Group With Previous Layer option and click OK.

This adjustment layer will alter the color cast of the object.

12. Turn on the Preview option in the Levels or Curves dialog box. Adjust the shadows and highlights so that the image appears to naturally fit into the background's lighting.

In this example, the Blue curve was adjusted so that the image would seem warmer and its highlights would look more yellow.

13. Select the Shadow layer in the Layers palette and click the Add Layer Mask button at the bottom of the Layers palette. Select the gradient tool and select the Black, White gradient. Apply a linear gradient to the layer mask with white at the base of the shadow and dark gray at the far edge.

The shadow will fade in the direction of the gradient vector. If the gradient makes the shadow too subtle, reapply using a lighter part of the gradient.

14. Select the Object layer in the Layers palette. Use the dodge or burn tool to correct other small lighting problems.

In this example, the left side of the elephant and its feet were darkened.

Transparent shadows

Adobe Illustrator 10 or later

Designers and illustrators commonly need semitransparent shapes for shadows that overlap other objects in their drawings. The Flat-color Shadow method creates a semitransparent shadow using solid colors and the Transparency palette. It's very quick and easy. The Gradient Shadow method creates a more subtle and realistic effect using transparency, the Multiply blending mode, and a little Gaussian blur.

Flat-color shadow

1. Make sure that the artwork is sized, painted, and positioned as you want it.

2. Option/Alt-click the New Layer button in the Layers palette to create a new layer. Name it Shadow. Move it directly beneath the layer of the object that will cast the shadow.

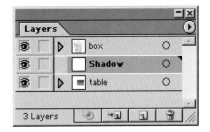

3. Create the shadow shape and fill it with a shadow color. Arrange the shadow so that it is in front of any object it shades but behind the object casting it.

Try to use a color other than black for your shadow. It makes the shadow look more interesting and realistic. In this example, a dusty purple was used.

4. With the Shadow layer still selected, display the Transparency palette. Choose Multiply as the blending mode and adjust the Opacity.

5. Deselect the shadow shape and evaluate the result. If you are satisfied, save the file.

To create a gradated, softer shadow, try the Gradient Shadow technique that follows.

Gradient shadow

1. Make sure that the artwork is sized, painted, and positioned as you want it.

2. Option/Alt-click the New Layer button in the Layers palette to create a new layer. Name it Shadow Gradient. Move it directly beneath the layer of the object that will cast the shadow.

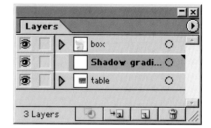

3. Create the shadow shape and arrange it so that the shadow is in front of the objects it will shade and behind the object casting it. Fill the shadow with the White, Black gradient in the Swatches palette.

4. Select the gradient tool in the toolbox. Use the tool to redirect the gradient so that the black area is closest to the object casting the shadow and the white area is farthest from the object.

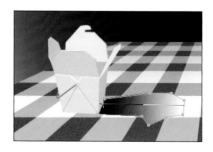

5. With the shadow shape still selected, change the blending mode to Multiply in the Transparency palette. Adjust the Opacity if necessary.

6. Choose View > Hide Edges to evaluate the adjustments without the visual distraction of the selection edges.

7. In the Gradient palette, click the black gradient slider to select it. Open the Color palette and use the palette menu to change the color mode from Grayscale to one of the color choices. Change the gradient stop from black to a different dark shadow color.

This example used a dark purple.

8. If desired, further adjust the shadow by moving the midpoint gradient slider to change the dark and light areas of the shadow.

If you move the slider toward the the dark stop, the shadow fades more quickly. If you move the slider toward the white stop, the shadow becomes darker and fades more slowly.

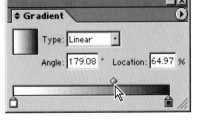

9. For a softer shadow, select the shadow shape and choose Effect > Blur > Gaussian Blur. Use a small amount of blur to keep the effect subtle.

If the edges don't look smooth enough, choose Effect > Document Raster Effects Settings and increase the resolution setting.

Gradients on a path

Adobe Illustrator 10 or later

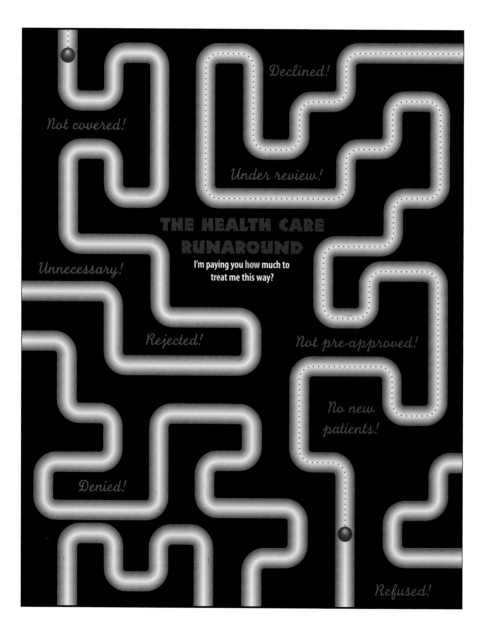

Need to create neon, rainbows, tubes, or pipes? Then this is the technique to use. First create an art brush from a gradient. (Create your own gradient or use one of the many gradients installed in your Gradient Libraries folder.) Then apply it to a path. One advantage to using the art brush gradient is that you can quickly and easily change its color. Another is that if you edit the path, the gradient automatically reflows along the new path.

1. Select the rectangle tool. Position the cursor in a blank area of the file, and click once. Enter the Width and Height amounts. The Width amount should be a few times larger than the Height. The Height amount should be the thickness that you want your path gradient to be.

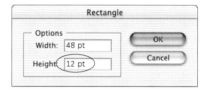

2. Fill the rectangle with the White, Black gradient, which is one of the default gradients found in the Swatches palette. Stroke the rectangle with None.

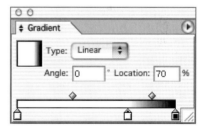

3. Choose Window > Gradient to display the Gradient palette. The White, Black gradient will appear in the palette. Click below the gradient bar to add a new color. Select white in the Color palette to fill the new stop with white. Position the new stop at the 70% location. If this is difficult, type in the value, and press Enter.

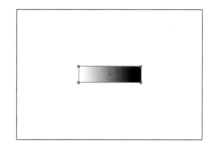

4. Select the far right stop on the gradient bar. Select 80% black in the Color palette.

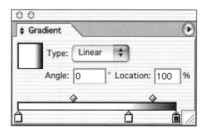

5. Select the leftmost stop on the gradient bar. Select 80% black in the Color palette. Change the angle to 90°.

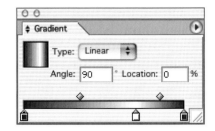

6. Evaluate the results. You should have a grayscale version of the tubular gradation you will eventually apply to a path. If you need to do any resizing or color editing, do it now.

You'll expand the gradient into shapes so that you can create an art brush in the next step.

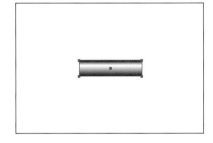

7. Choose Object > Expand to change the gradient into a series of shapes. The number of objects you specify will depend on the height of the rectangle. Click OK.

In this example, 50 objects were specified for a 12-point thick tube. You may need to experiment with this value to create the smoothest blend. Start with a ratio of 4 objects for each point of tube thickness.

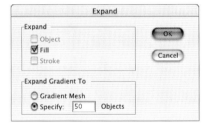

8. Choose Window > Pathfinder to display the Pathfinder palette. With the expanded gradient still selected, click the Crop button in the Pathfinder palette.

Expanding the gradient converts the rectangle into a mask for the blended shapes. The Crop command trims the shapes and removes the mask. Art brushes cannot contain masks.

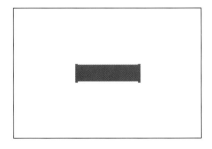

9. Use the pop-up menu on the Brushes palette menu to make sure that Show Art Brushes is selected. Click the New Brush button at the bottom of the palette, and select Art Brush as the type. Name the new brush, and select Tints and Shades as the Colorization method. Click OK.

10. Create a path to which you can apply the gradient art brush. Stroke it with the color that will be the main color of the tube gradient. Fill it with None if you want only the tube gradient to show.

Art brushes that have Colorization methods of Tints, Tints and Shades, or Hue Shift will use the color of a path's stroke, not its fill.

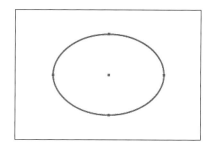

11. With the path still selected, click the gradient art brush that you just created in the Brushes palette. Save the file.

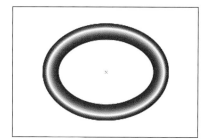

Variation 1: Replace steps 3 through 6 with the following: Fill the rectangle with the Rainbow gradient from the default set in the Swatches palette, and continue with step 7. When creating the art brush in step 9, use a Colorization method of None.

Variation 2: Replace the gradient stops in steps 3 through 5 with the following: Set the 0% and 100% locations to 100% white. Set the 70% location to 50% black and move it to the 50% location. Then continue with step 6.

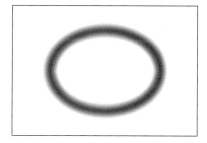

Stippling

Adobe Photoshop 7.0 or later
Adobe Illustrator 10 or later (optional)

Different colors spatter-painted or airbrushed on top of each other creates a rich textural look. Using several different colors for shadows instead of just black creates a richer effect. As an alternative, you can add dimension and character to your type or graphics using textured gradations. First build a different layer for each color you want to spatter onto your image. Then add a layer mask and texturize it. You'll end up with a multilayered file that is very versatile. You can experiment with different colors, layer modes, and textures as you lay one colored texture on top of another.

1. Create a basic design with flat shapes of color. Make a separate layer for each different colored object.

If you use graphics created in Illustrator, export them in the Photoshop (PSD) format. Choose the Write Layers option and open the file in Photoshop. Set the resolution depending on how coarse or fine you want the stipple texture. The higher the resolution, the finer the stipple texture.

2. Select the layer of the first graphic you want to texturize. Make a copy of that layer by Option/Alt-dragging it to the New Layer button at the bottom of the Layers palette. Name the new layer Texture 1. Select the Lock Transparent pixels option.

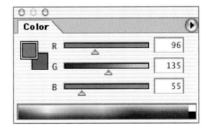

If the layer is a type layer, the transparent pixels will be locked automatically.

3. Choose a color that you want to stipple onto the base color of the original shape.

4. Fill the Texture 1 layer with the foreground color. A shortcut for filling with the foreground color is Option+Delete (Mac OS) or Alt+Backspace (Windows).

Don't worry about the color covering up the original. The stipple texture will be applied in the next few steps.

5. Option/Alt-click the Add Layer Mask button at the bottom of the Layers palette to add a layer mask to the Texture 1 layer.

Pressing the Option/Alt key fills the layer mask with black, which blocks out the new color until you change it.

6. With the layer mask still selected, choose Filter > Noise > Add Noise. Turn on the Preview option so that you can see the effect on your image. When you have the amount of color and texture that looks good with your graphic, click OK.

7. Evaluate the result. If you don't want to add any more stipple colors to this graphic, repeat steps 2 through 7 for any other layers in your file that need stippling. For multicolor stippling, continue with step 8.

You may be satisfied with adding just one color, but mixing at least two or three colors together produces a richer effect.

8. Repeat steps 2 through 5 and name the new layer Texture 2.

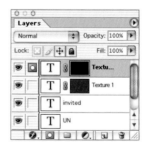

9. Reapply the Add Noise filter just as you did in step 6, but this time use a different amount. In this example, the Noise amount was increased to get more purple dots than green.

10. Repeat steps 8 and 9 for as many colors as you want to add. Stop and save the file, or continue with the next step if you want to create a stippled gradation.

Stippled gradients

1. Make a new layer and position it directly over the layer you want to stipple. Name the layer Gradient Texture 1.

In this example, a textured gradient will be added to the background. If you want the textured gradient applied to a shape on a layer, Option/Alt-click between the layers to create a clipping mask.

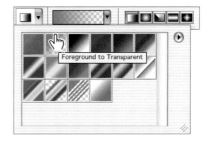

2. Change the foreground color to the color you want to use for the stippled gradation. Select the gradient tool in the toolbox. In the tool options bar, click the Linear Gradient button and click the arrow next to the gradient sample to display the gradient picker. Change the Gradient type to Foreground to Transparent.

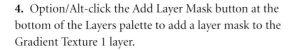

3. Apply a gradient to the Gradient Texture 1 layer with the gradient tool.

Don't worry if there is too much color at this point. You can control the amount of color added by how much noise you use in the next step.

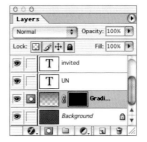

4. Option/Alt-click the Add Layer Mask button at the bottom of the Layers palette to add a layer mask to the Gradient Texture 1 layer.

5. With the layer mask still selected, choose Filter > Noise > Add Noise. Turn on the Preview option so that you can see the effect on your image. When you have the amount of color and texture that looks good with your graphic, click OK.

6. Evaluate the result. If you don't want to add any more stipple colors to this gradient, repeat steps 1 through 5 of this technique for any other gradients that need stippling. For multicolor stippling, continue with step 7.

Remember, stippling with at least two or three different colors together produces a richer effect.

7. Repeat steps 1 through 4 using a different foreground color and name the new layer Gradient Texture 2.

8. Reapply the Add Noise filter just as you did in step 5, but this time use a different amount. In this example, the Noise amount was decreased to get fewer red dots than green.

9. Add the stipple texture to the remaining elements in your design.

Shadows have color and texture, too, so don't forget to stipple the shaded areas with several colors instead of leaving them just black.

In this example, a 60% gray-blue drop shadow was added and its blending mode was set to Multiply.

2

Drawing

Custom borders

Adobe Illustrator 10 or later

One of the most useful things you can create with the Adobe Illustrator pattern brush is a border. Pattern brushes offer you the option of having corner designs that differ from the side designs. You also don't have to worry about calculating the size of the tile to fit your particular rectangle because Illustrator offers three Pattern Brush fit options. If you want to customize one of the pattern brushes provided in the several libraries that come on the CD, simply drag the tiles out of the Brushes palette onto your page and change the artwork to your taste. Then follow steps 7 through 14 to resave the tiles.

1. Select the rectangle tool and create a square large enough to contain the border corner artwork.

It doesn't matter what the fill and stroke are because this square will become a guide.

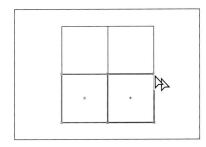

2. Choose View > Hide Bounding Box. With the selection tool, click on one of the left corner points and drag the square to the right, pressing Shift + Option/Alt as you drag. Once the left corner point aligns with the right one, release the mouse button and then the Shift and Option/Alt keys to create a copy.

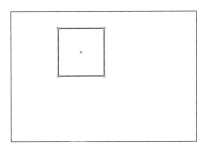

3. Select both of the squares. Click one of the corner top points, press Shift + Option/Alt, and drag the squares straight down. Once the top corner point aligns with the bottom one, release the mouse button and then the Shift and Option/Alt keys to create copies.

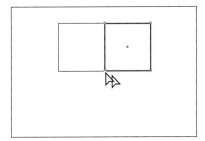

4. Select all four of the squares and choose View > Guides > Make Guides.

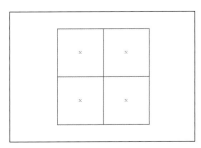

5. Create the artwork for the sides of the border in the upper right square guide.

The artwork should be just shapes or lines. Don't use unexpanded brush strokes because aligning them perfectly is nearly impossible. If you want to use a brush stroke, expand it first so you can use its points to align to the edges and center point of the pattern tile boundaries.

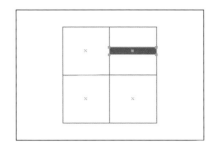

6. Select the rectangle tool and create a square the same size as the square guide. Fill and stroke the square with None. Choose Object > Arrange > Send to Back.

This invisible square will become the bounding box for the side pattern tile. It will also help you align the side tile with the corner tile.

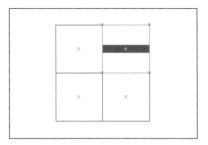

7. Select both the side artwork and its invisible bounding box. Choose New Brush from the Brushes palette menu. Select New Pattern Brush as the type, and click OK. The side tile artwork will appear in the Side Tile thumbnail. If you want the border to remain the same color, choose None for the Colorization method. Name the tile and click OK.

8. Choose Illustrator > Preferences > Smart Guides & Slices (OS X) or Edit > Preferences > Smart Guides & Slices (Mac OS and Windows) to set the Display Options. Turn on all of the Display Options. Then choose View > Smart Guides and make sure they are turned on.

You need to use guides to ensure that the tile art and corner art align perfectly.

9. With the side tile artwork still selected, select the reflect tool in the toolbox. Click once on the bottom left corner of the selected artwork (1). Press the Option/Alt key and then click a second time on the upper left corner of the top left guide box (2) to create a copy.

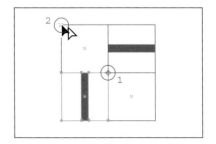

10. Create the corner artwork. Use the Smart Guides' Text Label Hints, Object Highlighting, and Construction Guides as aids in matching the points of the outer corner design to the side tile design. The side tiles should flow seamlessly into the outer corner tile.

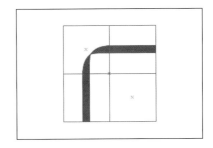

11. Repeat step 6 to create an invisible bounding box for the outer corner design.

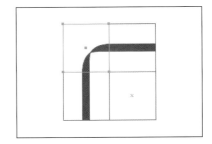

12. Select the outer corner tile artwork and its bounding box. Option/Alt-drag it into the Brushes palette and position it over the outer corner section of the new pattern brush you created in step 7. Release the mouse button, and then the Option/Alt key when you see the thick black border appear. Click OK in the Pattern Brush Options dialog box.

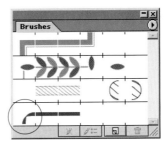

13. Repeat step 12 for the inner corner design, except Option/Alt-drag the design into the inner corner section in the Brushes palette. Usually the outer corner design works as the inner corner design as well. To create an inner corner for nonsymmetric borders, return to step 10. Rotate the outer corner tile art 90° and adjust it to match the side tile. Continue with step 11.

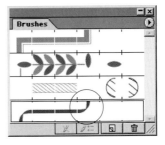

14. Once you've defined the sides and corners of the pattern brush, test it. Draw a shape and click the pattern brush name in the Brushes palette.

Notice in the example that shapes without corners were painted only with the side tile design. Corner tiles appear only on paths with corner points.

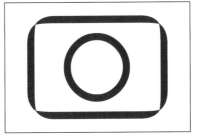

Drawing foliage

Adobe Illustrator 10 or later

Illustrator's symbolism tools are great for creating large areas of leaves, grass, and flowers. You can make an endless number of fields with just one symbol. In this technique you'll create a group of grass blade shapes and define it as a symbol. (You can do this with other types of foliage, too.) After you create a symbol set, you'll customize it so that when you've finished, you'll have a field of randomly placed blades of grass—shaded, scaled, and colored —just as in nature. You can use more than one symbol in a symbol set. Try making several symbols with different sizes, shapes, and colors of grass. Note that you can get excellent results if you use a pressure-sensitive tablet and stylus with this technique.

1. Create several grass blade shapes with the pen tool. Paint them a few different colors of green. Spread them out so that you can see white space between them. Select the blades of grass with the selection tool.

2. Choose Window > Symbols to display the Symbols palette. Click the New Symbol button at the bottom of the palette to create a new symbol from the selected artwork. If you want to name the symbol, double-click the thumbnail and name it Tall Grass.

3. Choose Window > Layers to display the Layers palette. Create a new layer, and name it Grass Field. Hide the layer on which you created the symbol artwork.

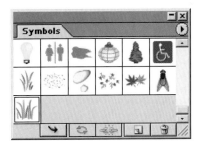

4. Double-click the symbol sprayer tool in the toolbox to open the Symbolism Tools Options dialog box. Select a diameter for the tool. In this example, because the illustration is small, a diameter of 36 pt was entered. Click OK.

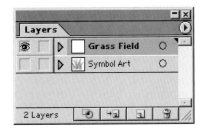

5. Use the symbol sprayer tool to create a small field of grass. As you press the mouse button and move the sprayer around the artwork, more blades of grass are created.

6. Display the Color palette, and select a green fill color that is not a part of the grass blade symbol art. You'll use this color in the next step to colorize the grass blades with the symbol stainer tool.

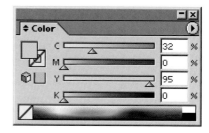

7. Select the symbol stainer tool in the toolbox. Gently paint over a few areas of the symbol set to change the colors of some of the grass blades.

8. Select the symbol sizer tool in the toolbox. Press the Option/Alt key and click over a few areas of the symbol set to reduce the size of the grass blades. Use the tool without the Option/Alt key to increase the size of the grass blades.

9. Select the symbol shifter tool in the toolbox. Drag over a few areas of the symbol set to move the blade symbols around. If you are satisfied with the artwork, save the file. If you want to add a style to parts of the symbol set, deselect the symbol set and continue with the next step.

Adding a style to the symbol set

1. To create a style and then add it to the symbol set, make sure that nothing is selected. Choose Window > Appearance to display the Appearance palette. Depending on what object was selected last, the palette may contain a Stroke or Fill color. If so, select the item in the Appearance palette and choose None.

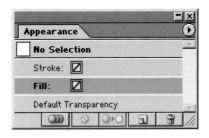

2. Choose Effect > Stylize > Drop Shadow to create a small shadow for the grass. Change the Opacity to 25%. Set the X and Y Offset value to 1 pt. Set Blur to 0 pt and select the Color option. Change the color to a dark green by clicking the color swatch and choosing a color in the Color Picker. Click OK twice to apply the shadow to the appearance.

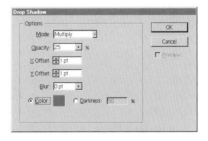

3. Choose Window > Transparency to display the Transparency palette. Choose either Multiply or Screen for the blending mode. Multiply will make the grass blades darker where they overlap other blades. Screen will make the blades lighter where they overlap.

4. Display the Styles palette by choosing Window > Styles. Drag the Appearance thumbnail onto the Styles palette. Double-click the style thumbnail and name the new style Grass Shadow. Click OK.

5. Select the symbol set in the artwork. Select the Grass Shadow style in the Styles palette. Select the symbol styler tool in the toolbox and gently stroke across the areas where you want shaded grass blades (or lightened ones if you used the Screen mode in step 3).

Quick 3-D boxes

Adobe Illustrator 10 or later

Illustrator's Smart Guide feature lets you quickly create objects at specific angles without rotating and shearing. Follow this technique and you'll learn how to create a three-dimensional box. Then you can use this technique to create a vast array of three-dimensional objects. Try making your drawings using some of the other angle choices available in the Smart Guides preferences. If you find that the Smart Guides are elusive and hard to find as you move the mouse around, change the Snapping Tolerance preference to a higher value.

1. Choose View > Smart Guides to turn the guides on. Then choose Illustrator > Preferences > Smart Guides & Slicing (OS X) or Edit > Preferences > Smart Guides & Slicing (Mac OS and Windows). Select 30° Angles for the Angle type. Turn on all four of the Display Options. If desired, adjust the Snapping Tolerance.

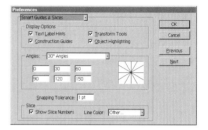

2. Choose Window > Info. Select the pen tool and click to make the bottom corner point (point A). Without clicking the mouse button, move the pen tool straight up along the Smart Guide 90° line until the Info palette displays the desired height of the front panel edge.

In this example, the height is 48 points.

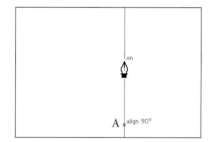

3. Click the pen tool at the desired distance to establish point B.

Be sure to click when the Smart Guide is displayed and when it indicates that the line is aligned at 90°.

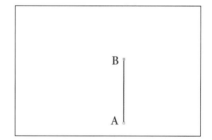

4. Without pressing the mouse button, drag the pen tool at an angle along the 150° Smart Guide. Look at the Info palette, and when the pen is positioned at the correct distance for the width of the front panel, click to set point C.

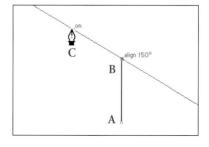

5. Drag the pen tool down to point A to instruct Illustrator that the next point will align with this corner point.

If you don't perform this step, you'll be guessing where on the 90° guide to place the bottom back corner point.

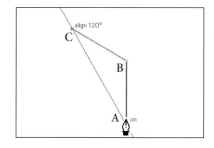

6. Drag the pen tool away from point A along the 150° Smart Guide. When you get close to the 90° guide that is aligned with point C, move the pen tool slowly until you see both guides appear at once. A text label should appear that says "intersect." Once this label appears, click to set point D.

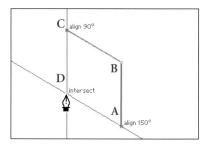

7. Click point A to close the path.

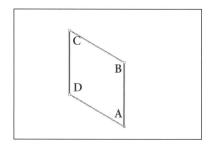

8. Deselect the front panel shape. Position the pen tool over point B and click to start the edge of the top panel.

Deselecting is important here because the pen tool will automatically remove the point if you click over a point on a selected path.

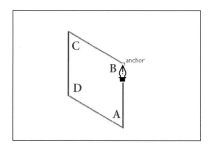

9. Click again on top of point C. Drag the pen tool out along the 30° Smart Guide the desired distance. Click the pen to establish point E of the top panel.

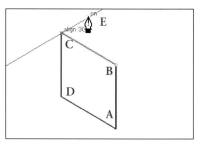

10. Drag the pen tool down to point B and then along the 30° Smart Guide until the intersection point appears. Click to set point F.

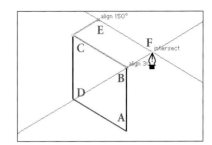

11. Click point B to close the top panel shape. Deselect the top panel and position the pen tool over point F. Click to establish the first corner point of the side panel.

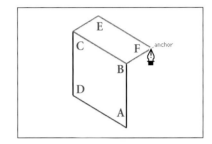

12. Position the pen tool over point B and click once. Move the pen tool down and click point A.

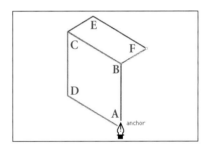

13. Without clicking, drag the pen tool up to point F and then drag down the 90° Smart Guide until you reach the intersection with the 30° Smart Guide. Click to establish point G at the right corner of the side panel.

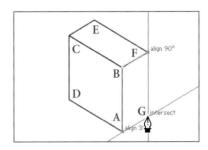

14. Click the top front corner point to close the side panel shape. Fill each panel with different colors or gradients to emphasize the three dimensions. Then save the file.

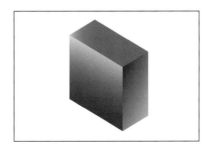

3-D packages

Adobe Illustrator 10 or later

Bella Linda Gourmet Foods

Olive Spread
Chopped Alfonso and Calabrese olives, capers, garlic and a touch of olive oil. Delicious spread on crackers or toast.
8 oz. jar $12.00

Tomato Paste
Pureéd sun-ripened Roma tomatoes. Great for pizza and pasta sauces.
8 oz. tube $4.00

Anchovy Paste
Pureéd Atlantic anchovies, sea salt and olive oil. A must for Caesar salad dressings.
4 oz. tube $5.00

You learned how to quickly draw a three-dimensional box on page 70. But what if you have a flat package design that needs to be transformed from two dimensions into three? Use Adobe Illustrator's precision tools to create isometric, axonometric, dimetric, and trimetric views from your two-dimensional artwork. The chart at the end of this technique provides the precise values needed for each type of three-dimensional drawing.

1. Create a flat view of your package, and then group the artwork for each panel. Using the examples shown on the facing page, choose the three panels on which you need to produce a perspective view and position them as indicated.

The three panels will be scaled, sheared, and rotated using the intersection of the three panels as the point of origin.

2. Select the top panel. Choose the scale tool and Option/Alt-click the intersection point to set the point of origin. The Scale dialog box opens.

3. Select the view you want to create from the chart on page 77. Click the Non-Uniform Scale option and enter the appropriate Vertical scale value for the top panel. Click OK.

This example used the value for the Trimetric 2 view.

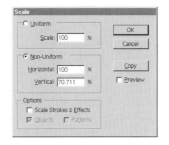

4. With the top panel still selected, select the shear tool and Option/Alt-click the intersection point. Enter the appropriate value for Horizontal Shear from the chart on the facing page.

This example used 45°.

5. Select the rotate tool, and Option/Alt-click the intersection point. Enter the rotate value indicated in the chart, and click OK.

This step makes the top panel appear to recede into space. In this example, the rotation angle was −15°.

6. Repeat steps 2 through 5 for the front panel. Be sure to use the numbers indicated for the front panel in the chart.

7. Repeat steps 2 through 5 for the side panel, using the corresponding set of numbers in the chart.

8. If the panels are stroked, zoom in very close on the corner joints to see whether the corners extend past the intersection point, as shown in this illustration. Identify which panels have this problem.

9. To fix the corners, use the direct-selection tool to select the panel edges. Select the Round Join option in the Stroke palette. To enhance the three-dimensional effect, paint the panels with slightly different shades and tints. Save the file.

This example shows the colors lightened on the top panel and darkened on the side panel.

View Style			Vertical Scale	Horizontal Shear	Rotate
Axonometric		**Top**	100.000%	0°	−45°
		Front	70.711%	−45°	−45°
		Side	70.711%	45°	45°
Isometric		**Top**	86.602%	30°	−30°
		Front	86.602%	−30°	−30°
		Side	86.602%	30°	30°
Dimetric		**Top**	96.592%	15°	−15°
		Front	96.592%	−15°	−15°
		Side	50.000%	60°	60°
Trimetric 1		**Top**	86.602%	30°	−15°
		Front	96.592%	−15°	−15°
		Side	70.711%	45°	45°
Trimetric 2		**Top**	70.711%	45°	−15°
		Front	96.592%	−15°	−15°
		Side	86.602%	30°	30°

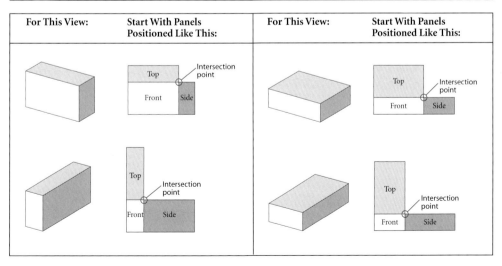

For This View:	Start With Panels Positioned Like This:	For This View:	Start With Panels Positioned Like This:

3-D bar charts

Adobe Illustrator 10 or later

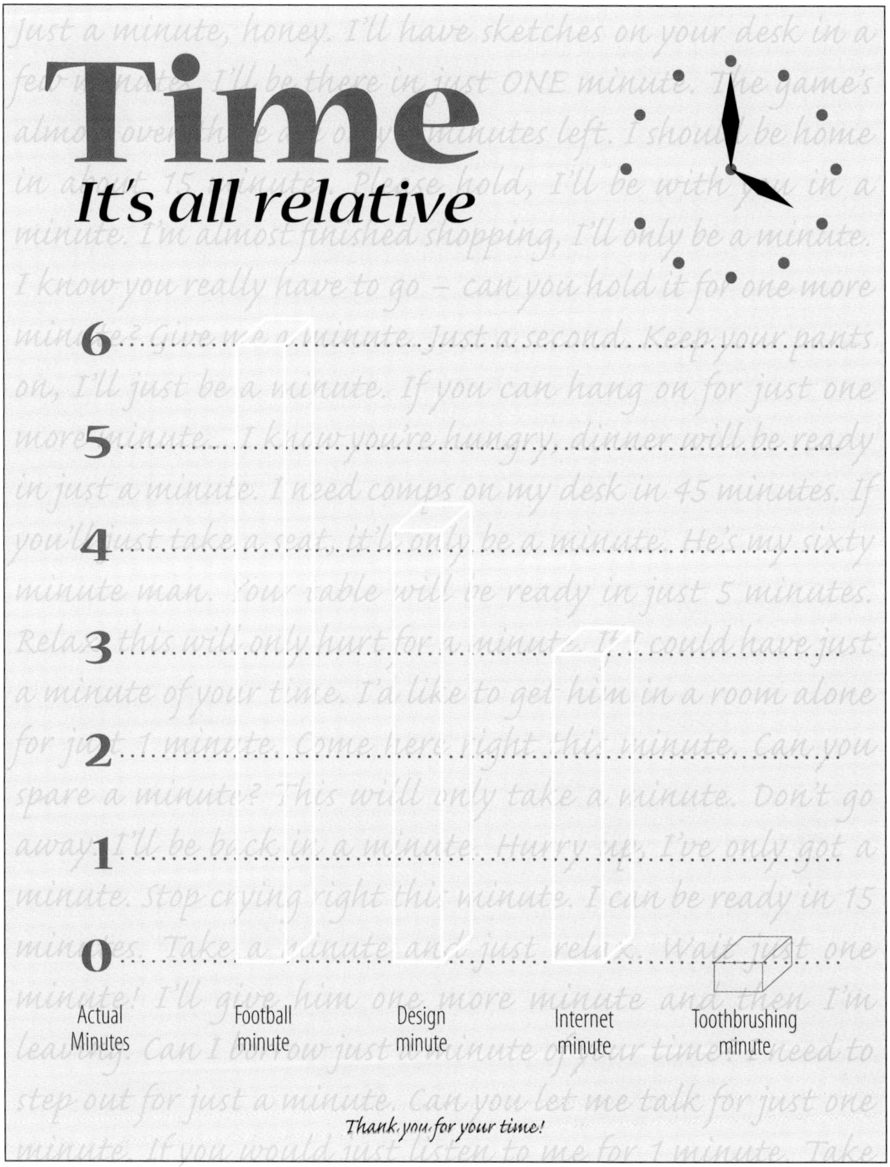

Time

It's all relative

6
5
4
3
2
1
0

Actual Minutes | Football minute | Design minute | Internet minute | Toothbrushing minute

Thank you for your time!

The graph tool in Adobe Illustrator creates flat, basic, unsophisticated graphs. But it is useful for calculating the correct ratio or size of the graphic elements. In this technique, start with a basic bar chart and create your own three-dimensional bar design. The third dimension adds a little more visual interest, but be careful of creating a design that's too elaborate. The purpose of a bar chart is to represent information that can be easily compared. Simple bar designs work best!

1. Create a grouped or stacked bar chart. Using the View menu, turn on both Snap to Point and Smart Guides.

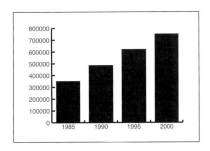

2. Use the direct-selection tool to select the smallest column in the graph. Copy it to the Clipboard and deselect the shape.

The smallest column is chosen to ensure that the top and side designs don't overlap when you make the sliding line in step 11.

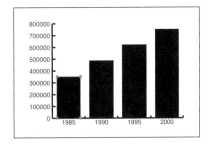

3. Create a new layer and call it Graph Design. Select that layer and paste the rectangle onto it. Hide the layer with the graph on it.

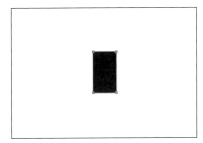

4. Paint the rectangle with a stroke and fill of None. Copy this version to the Clipboard.

This will become the bounding box for your bar design.

5. Choose Edit > Paste in Front to paste a copy of the bounding box directly on top of itself. Paint the rectangle with the color you want for the face of the three-dimensional bars.

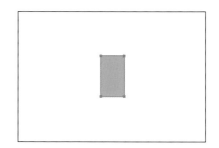

6. With the rectangle still selected, select the scale tool and Option/Alt-click the upper left corner point of the rectangle. Choose Non-Uniform scale and enter a Horizontal value of 100% and a Vertical value of −20%. Click Copy. Paint the top with a different color.

This shape will become the top of the three-dimensional bar.

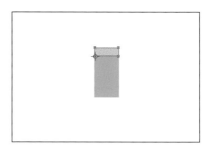

7. Select the shear tool and click once on the same upper left point you clicked in step 6. This sets the point of origin. Then click the right top point of the top rectangle, press and hold down the Shift key, and drag along the 0° Smart Guide. Release the mouse button and then the Shift key when you are satisfied with the shear angle.

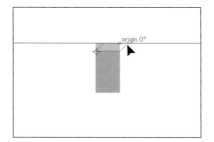

8. Choose the selection tool. Click one of the left corner points of the sheared top rectangle and drag to the right. Hold down the Shift and Option/Alt keys to make a copy and constrain it along the 0° Smart Guide. When you reach the corresponding right corner point, release the mouse button and then the Shift and Option/Alt keys.

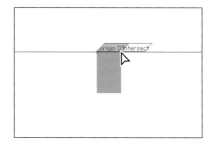

9. Use the direct-selection tool to select the two rightmost anchor points of the copy you just made. Click and drag the front right point down until it snaps to the lower right corner point of the bar. Paint the side of the column with a different color.

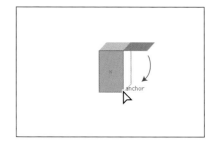

10. Use the pen or line segment tool to draw a horizontal line that intersects the column design. Position it between the top and bottom corner points. Select the line and the bar design and choose Object > Group.

This line will be the sliding boundary—a line below which the design will be vertically scaled in a graph. The area above the line won't change.

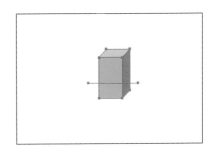

11. Use the direct-selection tool and select only the horizontal sliding line. Choose View > Guides > Make Guides.

The guide is grouped with the bar design. Even though the Lock Guides option may be turned on, the guide will still be selected when the group is selected.

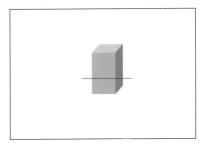

12. Select the group and choose Object > Graph > Design. Click the New Design button. Click the Rename button if you want to name the design something other than the default name. Click OK.

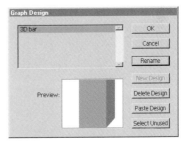

13. Hide the Graph Design layer in the Layers palette. Show the layer containing the bar graph. Select it, and choose Object > Graph > Column. Select the new column design, and choose Sliding as the Column Type. Click OK.

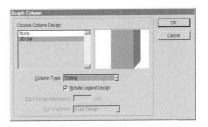

14. Choose View > Guides > Hide Guides to evaluate the results.

Adjust the layering of the axis lines or bars if necessary. Use the direct-selection tool to select the shapes or lines, and use the Arrange menu to reposition them. You can also change the type style and copy at this point.

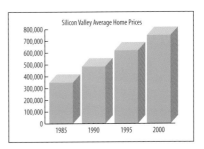

Shaded spheres

Adobe Photoshop 7.0 or later

COMMON CHEMICAL COMPOUNDS

Compound	Name	Molecule model
H_2O	Water	
NH_3	Ammonia	
H_2O_2	Hydrogen Peroxide	
CO_2	Carbon Dioxide	

Here are two different ways to make spheres in Photoshop—using gradients or layer styles. You can create shaded spheres using the gradient fill tool. The advantages to using a gradient are that you can position the highlight wherever you want and you can create many spheres of varying sizes with the same gradient. The disadvantage is that each time you want to change the color of your sphere you need to make a new gradient. The second technique uses layer styles. Once you've created your layer style you can use it over and over to create all different colored spheres. The disadvantages to this method are that you can only have the highlight in the center and you may need to adjust the settings for spheres of different sizes.

Gradient method

1. Open a new or existing file and create a new layer. Name the layer Sphere.

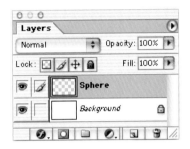

2. Select the elliptical marquee tool. Press the Shift key and draw a circle.

If you want to draw the circle from the center point, hold down the Option/Alt key as you start to draw.

3. Select the gradient tool in the toolbox. Then click the Radial Gradient button in the tool options bar.

4. Click the gradient sample to display the Gradient Editor dialog box. Use a highlight color at one end and a shadow color at the opposite end. Place a solid color at the 50% point on the gradient slider. Click the stop, and then click the Color swatch in the Stops section to change the colors. Name the gradient Sphere and click New to save it as a Preset. Click OK.

5. Click the arrow to the right of the gradient swatch to display the pop-up gradient palette and choose Sphere from the Gradient Picker. Position the radial gradient tool inside the circle selection at the point where you want the highlight. Click and drag to the edge of the selection and release the mouse button. Deselect the sphere.

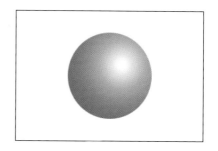

If you are satisfied with the result, save the file.

Layer Styles method

1. Open a new or existing file and create a new layer. Name the layer Sphere.

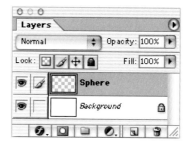

2. Select the elliptical marquee tool. Press the Shift key and draw a circle. Choose a color from the Color palette and fill the selection with that color. Deselect the circle.

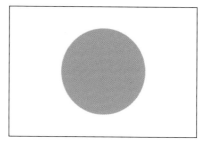

3. Click the Add Layer Style button in the Layers palette and select Inner Shadow. Make sure that the Preview box is checked. Adjust the Distance and Size settings until your sphere looks like the example. The amounts will vary depending on the size and resolution of the sphere. In this example, Distance = 11 px, Size = 54 px, and the angle is −164° for a 1-inch sphere at a resolution of 144 ppi.

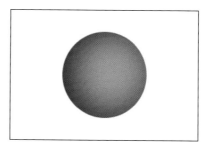

4. With the Layer Styles dialog box still open, click the arrow next to the contour to display the Contour picker. Select the Gaussian contour. (Hold your pointer over a contour thumbnail and its name will appear.) Click the Layer Styles dialog box to close the pop-up palette. Do not click OK yet.

5. From the Styles list, click the words "Inner Glow" to apply the effect and display its options. Click the color swatch to open the Color Picker. Change the glow color to white. Set the Technique to Precise and the Source to Center. Adjust the Size amount until you have a white highlight in the center of your sphere.

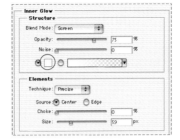

6. Vary settings depending on the diameter and resolution of your sphere. For this example, the Inner glow size was set to 59 px. Once you are satisfied with the effect, click OK.

7. Note whether the shading and highlights have flattened the original color in the sphere. You can adjust for this now. In the Layers palette menu, choose Duplicate Layer to duplicate the Sphere layer.

8. Remove the effects from the Sphere Copy layer by dragging its Effects sublayer to the Trash button at the bottom of the Layers palette.

Change the layer blending mode to Soft Light. Adjust the Opacity if necessary. If the gradient is banded, you may need to change colors.

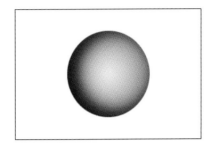

9. To change the color of the sphere quickly, turn on the Lock Transparent Pixels option for the Sphere and Sphere copy layers. Then choose different colors and fill the layers until you are satisfied with the result.

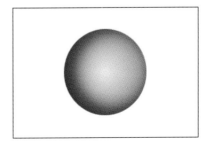

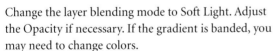

Perspective grids in Photoshop

Adobe Photoshop 7.0 or later

You can create a perspective grid in Photoshop that helps you match the perspective of imported graphics and images to that of the background image. This technique is especially helpful with images that contain strong perspective lines. To create the grid, you draw paths that define the vanishing points and horizon line of the image. Then you draw grid lines for positioning and sizing the imported artwork. Once the grid is created, you distort the imported image to align with the grid lines. Don't worry if the guidelines reach outside of the image; the pen tool displays outside the image in Full Screen mode.

1. Open a background file.

2. Option/Alt-click the New Layer button in the Layers palette and name the layer Guidelines.

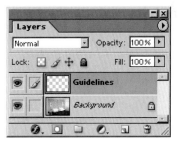

3. Select the pen tool in the toolbox. Click the Paths button in the tool options bar. Select the Full Screen Mode with Menu Bar button at the bottom of the toolbox. Zoom out and draw two paths that follow the perspective lines in your image. Use the direct-selection tool to pull out the endpoints of the lines to a point where they intersect. This is referred to as a vanishing point.

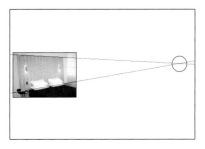

4. Create the first point of a new line, hold down the Shift key, and click the second point to draw a horizontal line. Use the direct-selection tool to move it until it intersects the vanishing point.

This is the horizon line.

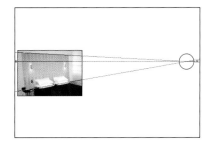

5. Draw additional guidelines to help create the perspective for positioning additional images or graphics.

In this example, additional lines were drawn as guides for a painting that will be placed on the headboard.

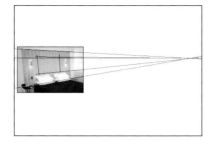

6. Select the Work Path, if it is not already selected, in the Paths palette, and then choose Save Path from the palette menu. Name the path Perspective Grid.

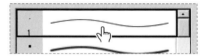
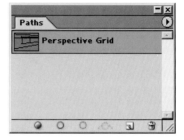

7. Select the pencil tool in the toolbox. Choose Window > Brushes to display the Brushes palette. Select the Hard Round 1-pixel brush.

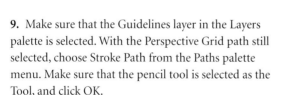

8. Choose Window > Color to display the Color palette. Select a very bright color to stroke the guidelines. Choose a color that will show up well against your background file.

The guidelines will not print; they serve only as references while building the image.

9. Make sure that the Guidelines layer in the Layers palette is selected. With the Perspective Grid path still selected, choose Stroke Path from the Paths palette menu. Make sure that the pencil tool is selected as the Tool, and click OK.

10. Click the blank area below the Perspective Grid path in the Paths palette to deselect the paths. If the lines don't show up well on your image, continue with step 11. If the lines show up well, skip to step 12.

11. Select a new color in the Color palette. Turn on the Lock Transparent Pixels option for the Guidelines layer. Choose Edit > Fill, and fill the layer with the new foreground color. Continue trying this until you find a color that contrasts well with your image.

12. Create, place, or paste the image to be transformed into perspective.

13. Choose Edit > Free Transform. To distort freely, press the Command/Ctrl key as you drag one of the corner points to its desired location. Use the guidelines as references to position each of the corner points of the transform bounding box. Once the image has been scaled and distorted to fit the guidelines, press Return/ Enter to perform the transformation.

14. Hide or delete the Guidelines layer. If necessary, adjust the layer blending mode or opacity of the transformed image to make it fit visually with the Background layer. Repeat steps 5 through 14 for any other objects that you add to the image.

Perspective grids in Illustrator

Adobe Illustrator 10 or later

This technique shows how to use guidelines and Smart Guides to create perspective drawings. You'll set up the perspective grid and create the flat shapes that appear on the picture plane. Then you'll draw the sides of the objects along the gridlines and create any receding copies of the elements within the object using the scale tool. The final part of this technique shows how to create blends for repeating horizontal or vertical details.

Drawing objects in perspective

1. Create a simple 1-point perspective grid. First draw a rectangle to denote the picture plane (A) and a horizon line (B). Then decide where the vanishing point (C) will be. Draw straight lines from the vanishing point past the corners of the rectangle. The lines should intersect the corners of the picture plane.

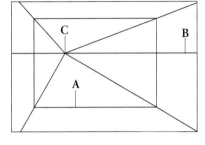

2. Select the lines and rectangle and choose View > Guides > Make Guides.

To use a more complex, premade grid, choose File > Open, nagivate to the Illustrator application folder, and then follow this path: Sample Files > Template Samples > 1ptPerspectiveGrid.ai.

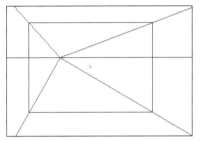

3. Create the background shapes. Remember to use the horizon line guide when creating the sky and earth or floors and walls.

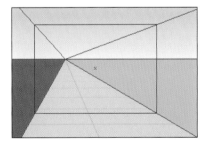

4. Create a new layer for objects that sit above the background shapes. Check the View menu to see that the Snap to Point option is turned on. Create and fill the shape for the front plane of the first object in your drawing. Draw a flat shape with no distortion. Deselect the shape.

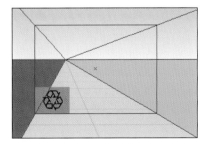

5. Select the pen tool and draw a line from one of the corner points of the picture plane to the vanishing point. While the line is still selected, choose View > Guides > Make Guides. Repeat this step for key points and angles on the front plane.

This example shows guides added to create the bottom, back, and right side of the box.

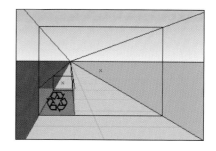

6. Draw the sides of the object using the guides. Paint the sides with colors slightly different from the front shape. Repeat steps 4 through 6 for each new object you create. Continue with the next technique, Transforming in Perspective, to transform objects into perspective.

This example used the Layers palette to arrange the sides, bottom, and back of the box behind the box front.

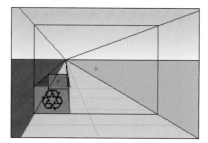

Transforming in perspective

1. To create multiple shapes that recede toward the vanishing point, create the frontmost shape using the guidelines and select it. Choose View and turn on Smart Guides. Choose Illustrator > Preferences > General (OS X) or Edit > Preferences > General (Mac OS and Windows) and select the Scale Strokes & Effects option.

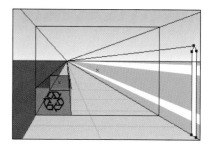

2. Select the scale tool, and then click the vanishing point once to set the origin point. Move the pointer to a point on the selected shape that intersects one of the guides. Drag the point along the guideline toward the vanishing point; then press the Option/Alt key. Release the mouse button and then the Option/Alt key to make a copy.

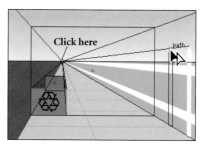

3. To make additional receding copies, choose Object > Transform > Transform Again for as many copies as you need.

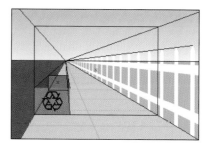

Blending in perspective

1. To create evenly spaced lines or shapes on the sides of objects, draw the frontmost shape using the perspective guidelines.

In this example, drawing a shape—instead of stroking a line—ensured that the top and bottom of the line were angled properly.

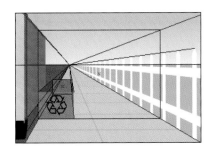

2. Use the scale tool as instructed in step 2 of the preceding technique on page 92 to create a smaller copy of the line or shape at the far end of the surface.

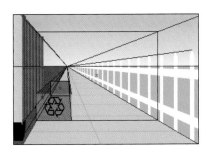

3. Select both lines or shapes, and choose Object > Blend > Make.

4. With the blend still selected, choose Object > Blend > Blend Options. Select Specified Steps for the Spacing and try different numbers of steps until you are satisfied with the effect. Click OK.

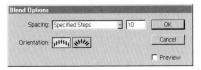

5. Add other objects to complete the illustration using the guides, the vanishing point, and the horizon line as aids in their construction.

For best results, use layers for each different object. Include an object's guidelines with its layer to keep the drawing organized.

Seals, stars, spheres, and links

Adobe Illustrator 10 or later

Scalloped seals

1. Select the ellipse tool, press and hold down the Shift key, and draw a circle. Holding down the Shift key makes the object you draw a perfect circle.

2. Choose Object > Path > Add Anchor Points. Reapply the Add Anchor Points command until you have the number of points you want.

In this example, the command was applied three times.

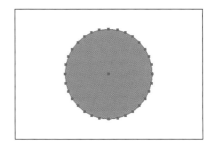

3. Choose Filter > Distort > Pucker & Bloat. Select the Preview option box and enter a negative number if you want the points on the outer edge of the circle. Click OK.

In this example, a value of –5% was used.

Scallop tool method: To change a circle into a scalloped seal quickly, use the scallop tool located in the warp tool group.

Double-click the scallop tool. Enter a brush size 12 points larger than the circle. Set the Intensity to 20% and Complexity to 8. Click the scallop tool cross hair on the center, of the circle. The longer you press the mouse button, the more extreme the result.

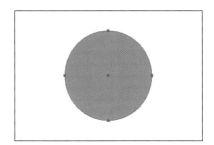

These techniques are quick, easy ways to draw little graphics often needed by designers and illustrators. The Scalloped Seals and Three-dimensional Stars techniques use a combination of Illustrator commands. The Quick Spheres technique is a fast way to make a sphere without a 3-D drawing program. You can't overlap stroked shapes easily, so use the Pathfinder palette to create interlocking shapes with just a few clicks.

Three-dimensional stars

1. Select the star tool, and click once in the document. Enter 4 in the Points field, and click OK. Choose Select > Deselect.

In this example, a value of 40 points for Radius 1 and 20 points for Radius 2 was used.

2. Using the View menu, turn on the Smart Guides and Snap to Point commands. Select the pen tool, and draw horizontal, vertical, and diagonal lines across the star between the anchor points. Use the Smart Guides to help you locate the anchor points.

It's a good idea to stroke the lines with a contrasting color to check alignment. The stroke color will disappear in the next step.

3. Choose Window > Pathfinder to display the Pathfinder palette. Select the star and all the intersecting lines. Click the Divide button in the Pathfinder palette to slice the star into separate shapes.

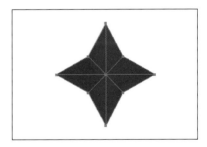

4. Select the direct-selection tool, hold down the Shift key, and select every other triangle in the star. Fill them with contrasting colors.

For best results, use a dark color for the shaded areas and a lighter value for the highlighted areas. To change color saturation quickly, in the Color palette hold the Shift key while dragging a CMYK or RGB slider.

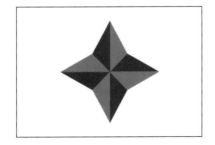

Quick spheres

1. Select the ellipse tool, press the Shift key, and drag to create a circle.

2. Choose Window > Gradient or click the Gradient tab to display the Gradient palette. Create a new gradient with the highlight color on the left side of the gradient slider and the shadow color on the right. Choose Radial for the Type.

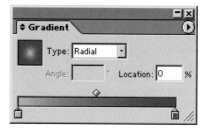

3. Select the circle, if deselected, and fill it with the radial gradient.

By default, the highlight color (the leftmost on the Gradient Palette slider) is in the center of the circle.

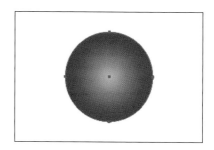

4. Select the gradient tool. Drag from the point where you want the highlight to the point where you want the shadow to begin.

5. In the Gradient palette, drag the diamond above the gradient slider to increase or decrease the amount of highlight in the sphere then deselect.

In this example, the diamond was moved from the 50% position to the 60% position to increase the size of the highlight.

Interlocking stroked objects

1. Select the objects that you want to link. Don't worry about adding the stroke yet— you'll do it at the end.

2. With the objects still selected, choose Window > Pathfinder to display the Pathfinder palette. Click the Divide button to define the overlapping color areas as separate shapes.

3. Determine how the links should be arranged visually to create the interlocking effect. Use the direct-selection tool and Shift-select the shapes you want to fill with one color. Click the Add to Shape Area button in the Pathfinder palette to join the selected shapes into one shape. Paint with the appropriate color.

4. While the shape is still selected, click the Expand button in the Pathfinder palette.

This creates a shape that can be stroked in the next step.

5. Repeat steps 3 and 4 for all interlocking objects in your artwork. Adjust the fill and stroke attributes of the objects.

Map symbols

Adobe Illustrator 10 or later

Use the Symbols palette for maps or any illustrations that require several copies of the same artwork. You simply place as many instances of a symbol as you want. The advantage to using symbols is that you can make changes quickly and easily to all the symbols in the file at once. Or you can select and change individual symbol instances without affecting all the others. This technique is a real time-saver for mapmakers. Once you've mastered using the Symbols palette here, try "Drawing Foliage" on page 66 for another way to use symbols.

1. Create a symbol or graphic that you want to repeat several times on your map. Select the symbol artwork.

2. Choose Window > Symbols to display the Symbols palette. Drag the selected artwork onto the Symbols palette. When you see the thick, black border inside the palette, release the mouse button.

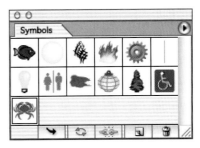

3. Double-click the symbol to open the Symbol Options dialog box, and name the new symbol. Click OK.

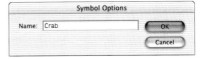

4. Open or create your illustration. Make it the Background layer of your artwork.

5. Click the Place Symbol Instance button at the bottom of the Symbols palette. This places one symbol instance in the center of your window.

If you want to control exactly where the symbol is placed, drag the symbol from the Symbols palette onto the artwork directly.

6. Continue placing symbols in each place you want the symbol to appear. Save the file. If you want to edit the symbol, continue with the next step.

You can also Option/Alt-drag and move an existing symbol instance in the artwork to make a copy and leave the original behind.

Editing a symbol

1. Select one of the symbol instances in your artwork.

2. Click the Break Link to Symbol button at the bottom of the Symbols palette.

You can use the Transform tools on a symbol instance or perform operations in the Appearance, Transparency, or Styles palette without breaking the link. But you can't edit the paths or change the colors without breaking the link.

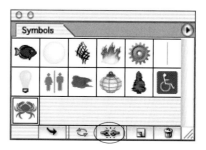

3. Create the new or altered symbol.

This example shows the color of the crab changed.

4. To replace the symbol with the newly edited version, select the new or altered symbol. Then select the original symbol in the Symbols palette, and choose Redefine Symbol from the Symbols palette menu.

The symbol is changed and all of its instances are updated with the new symbol.

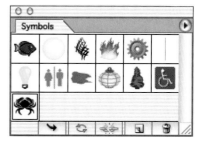

5. Save the file. If you are satisfied with your artwork, continue adding symbols. If you want to edit individual symbol instances, continue with the next step.

Editing symbol instances

1. Select one of the symbol instances in your artwork. Zoom in on the artwork, if necessary.

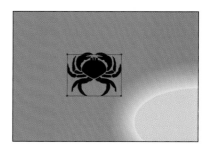

2. Use any of the transform tools, or perform an operation in the Appearance, Transparency, or Styles palette on the symbol instance.

Any of these operations can be performed on a symbol instance without breaking its link to the original symbol. In this example, the symbol instance was scaled and its opacity was set to 25%.

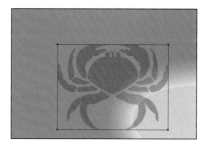

3. When you are satisfied with the changes, save the file.

Remember, you can use your symbols in other illustrations. To load the symbols used in another file, choose Window > Symbol Libraries > Other Library and open the file containing the symbols you want. A small palette will appear with the imported symbols in it.

3 Patterns and Textures

Simple patterns

Adobe Illustrator 10 or later

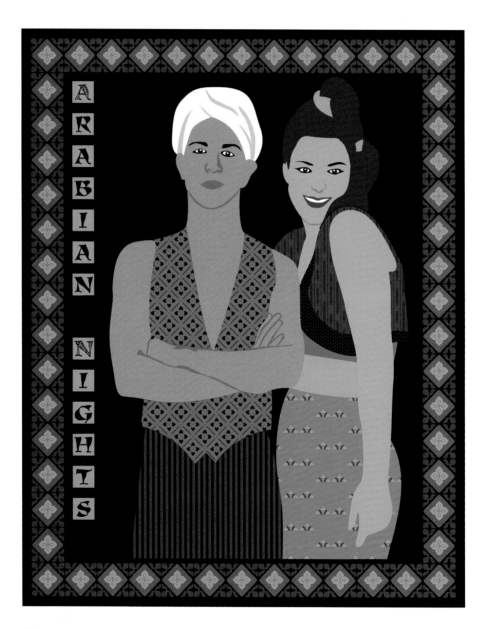

The simplest way to construct a pattern tile is to draw any graphic object and surround it with a rectangle placed in the background. This procedure describes how to take it a step further and create dense patterns that tile perfectly by positioning copies of the graphic in each corner of the background rectangle. Once you've created the basic pattern tile, you can transform it with any of the transformation tools. You can also make copies of the tile and create different color variations for design experimentation.

1. Select the rectangle tool and create a rectangle the size you want your pattern tile to be. For the most efficient printing and previewing, try to keep it between 1 and 2 inches square.
Note: Do not use the rounded rectangle tool for this step. The rectangle must have square corners.

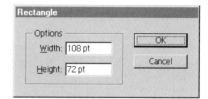

2. Fill the rectangle with the background color of your pattern. If you want the pattern to have a transparent background, fill and stroke it with None. If you want a solid background, stroke it with None.

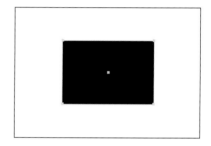

3. Create or copy and paste the artwork that you want to use as a repeating element in your pattern. Check the View menu to make sure that the Snap to Point and Smart Guides options are turned on.

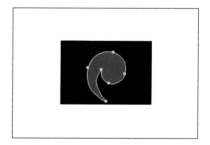

4. Skip this step if the element is the correct size for the pattern. If the element needs to be scaled, select the scale tool in the toolbox and scale the element.

The element must be small enough that copies can fit in the center and in each of the four corners without touching each other.

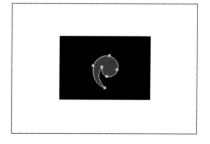

5. Choose Window > Attributes to display the Attributes palette. With the object selected, click the Show Center button to display the center point of the element.

6. Use the selection tool and grab the element by the center point. Drag it until it snaps to the upper left corner point of the rectangle. Don't release the mouse button until the pointer becomes a white arrowhead, indicating that the points have snapped.

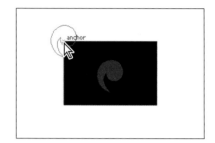

7. Grab the element again by its center point. Begin to drag it, and then press the Shift and Option/Alt keys to constrain and copy it. Drag until it snaps to the upper right corner point of the rectangle. Don't release the mouse button until the cursor becomes a white arrowhead, and the intersect hint appears. Release the mouse button and then the Shift and Option/Alt keys.

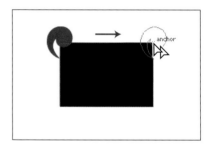

8. Select both top elements. Grab the right element by its center point. Begin to drag it down, and then press the Shift and Option/Alt keys. Drag until it snaps to the lower right corner point of the rectangle. Release the mouse button and then the Shift and Option/Alt keys.

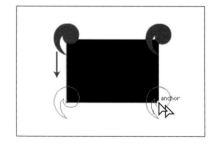

9. Place any additional graphics you want within the rectangle. Make sure that these elements don't overlap the rectangle edges. If they do, the pattern won't tile correctly.

In this example, a rotated version of the element was added and its center point was placed over the center point of the rectangle.

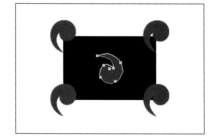

10. If you are already using a transparent rectangle as a background, skip to step 12. If your rectangle is stroked or filled, select the rectangle. Choose Edit > Copy and, while the rectangle is still selected, choose Edit > Paste in Back. Do not deselect yet.

It won't look like it, but you now have two rectangles stacked on top of each other.

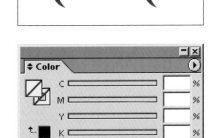

11. With the backmost rectangle still selected, paint it with a stroke and fill of None.

This invisible rectangle will become the bounding box for the pattern tile. It defines the edges of the tile.

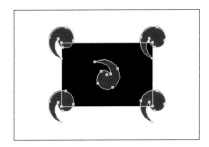

12. Select the selection tool in the toolbox and marquee-select both the rectangles and all of the pattern elements.

13. Choose Edit > Define Pattern. Name your pattern and click OK. The new pattern tile will appear in the Swatches palette.

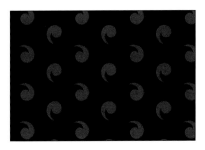

14. Create a shape, and then click the tile you just created in the Swatches palette to fill the shape with your new pattern.

Texture patterns

Adobe Illustrator 10 or later

You can create the effect of an uneven texture by constructing a pattern that appears irregular when it tiles. To achieve this effect, the edges of the pattern tile must match up perfectly so that the tiling creates one continuous texture. These textures take time to finesse, so once you've got a tile that works, try making different versions of it with different colors and stroke weights. If you need something quick, start with some premade tiles by loading the Pattern Samples libraries that came with your program. Then customize the tile for your own needs.

1. Use the rectangle tool to create a rectangle the size you want your pattern tile to be.

For the most efficient printing and previewing, try to keep it between 1 and 2 inches square.

Note: Do not use the rounded rectangle tool for this step. The rectangle must have square corners.

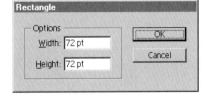

2. Fill the square with the background color of your pattern. If you want the pattern to have a transparent background, fill and stroke it with None. Begin drawing the texture with just the shapes or lines that intersect the left side of the square. Select the square and the texture.

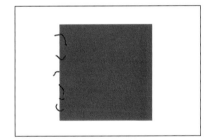

3. Check the View menu to make sure that the Snap to Point and Smart Guides options are turned on. Position the pointer on the lower left corner of the square. Begin dragging the artwork to the right; then press the Shift and Option/Alt keys to constrain and leave a copy. When the cursor snaps to the lower right corner point, release the mouse button and then the Shift and Option/Alt keys.

4. Select the right square and delete it.

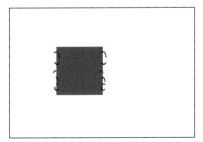

5. Continue drawing your texture by adding shapes or lines that intersect only the top of the square. When you have finished, select the rectangle and the top texture only.

6. Position the pointer on the upper right corner of the square. Begin dragging the artwork down; then press the Shift and Option/Alt keys to constrain the move and leave a copy. When the cursor snaps to the lower right corner point, release the mouse button and then the Shift and Option/Alt keys.

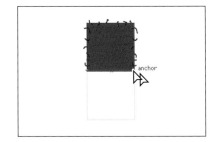

7. Select the lower square and delete it.

8. Fill in the middle of the square with your texture. Be careful not to intersect any of the square's edges or corners.

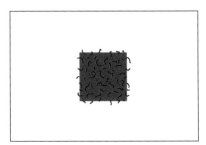

9. For a more varied texture, try using more than one color for the texture elements. If you repaint any edge pieces, be sure to paint the corresponding edge piece on the opposite side the same way.

Subtle color differences enhance the illusion that this is a texture instead of a repeating pattern.

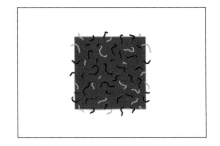

10. If you are already using a transparent square as a background, skip to step 12. If your square is stroked or filled, select the square. Choose Edit > Copy and, while the square is still selected, choose Edit > Paste in Back. Do not deselect yet.

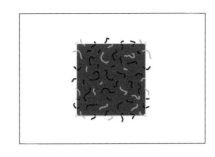

You now have two squares stacked on top of each other. One becomes a bounding box.

11. With the backmost square still selected, paint it with a stroke and fill of None.

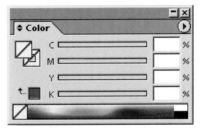

12. Select the squares and the texture elements. Choose Edit > Define Pattern. Name your pattern and click OK. The new pattern swatch will appear in the Swatches palette.

13. Create a large rectangle and select the pattern in the Swatches palette to fill the rectangle with the new pattern. Zoom out and look for places in the texture that create an obvious repeating pattern. If necessary, return to the pattern tile and adjust the artwork to smooth out obvious holes or clumps. The goal is to get a smooth, even texture with no obvious repetition.

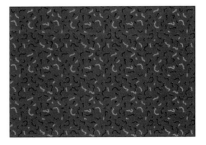

Variation: Select the pattern tile from step 10 and choose Filter > Colors > Invert Colors. Then continue with step 11.

Once you've got a texture that works, create different color versions so that you can use the texture more than once.

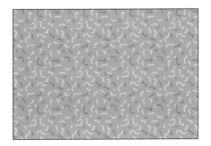

Illustrator pattern tiles in Photoshop

Adobe Photoshop 7.0 or later
Adobe Illustrator 10 or later

Illustrator comes with several libraries full of hundreds of pattern tiles that can be used in Photoshop. You can find a small number of the pattern tiles in the PostScript Patterns folder in the Photoshop application folder. This technique describes how to use these Illustrator pattern tiles or pattern tiles you've created using the "Simple Patterns" and "Texture Patterns" techniques on pages 104 and 108, in Photoshop. You'll use Illustrator to perfect the artwork so that it tiles seamlessly. Then you'll apply the pattern to your image in Photoshop and use layer blending modes and effects to enhance it.

1. Create a new Illustrator file. Follow the Simple Patterns technique on page 104 or drag a pattern from the Swatches palette onto the page.

To access a pattern library, choose Window > Swatch Libraries > Other Libraries, navigate to the application's Presets > Patterns folder, and open a pattern file. The tile artwork contains a bounding rectangle that is filled and stroked with None.

2. If desired, change the stroke or fill color in the pattern tile.

In this example, the stroke color was changed to 50% black because the pattern will be used to texturize an illustration in Photoshop.

3. Use the direct-selection tool to select the bounding rectangle of the pattern tile. Choose Edit > Copy, deselect everything, and then choose Edit > Paste in Front.

If the rectangle is filled, it will cover up your tile graphics. Don't worry about the fill obscuring the graphics; in the next step, you will convert the top rectangle to crop marks, and the fill will disappear.

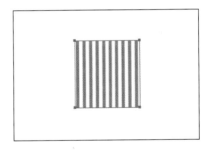

4. With the rectangle selected, choose Object > Crop Marks > Make. Save the file.

In order for Photoshop to import the tile art so that it tiles perfectly, you must create crop marks that are the same size and position as the pattern bounding box.

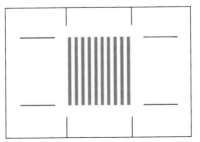

5. In Photoshop, open the Illustrator file you just saved. If you'll use the pattern tile with other Photoshop files, open the file in the same mode as those files. If your pattern has stripes or plaids at 90° angles, deselect the Anti-aliased option.

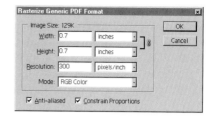

If you're unsure of your file's mode or resolution, use the File Browser in Photoshop to find that information before you open the pattern tile.

6. Choose Edit > Define Pattern. Name it with a .ai file extension and click OK.

The pattern is now available to be used whenever the Pattern Picker is displayed.

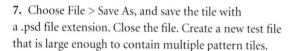

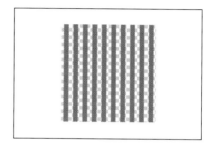

7. Choose File > Save As, and save the tile with a .psd file extension. Close the file. Create a new test file that is large enough to contain multiple pattern tiles.

If you open the new file in a different mode than the pattern tile, Photoshop will convert it.

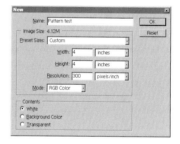

8. Choose Edit > Fill, and then choose Pattern from the Use menu. Click the arrow next to the pattern swatch to open the Pattern Picker. Select the pattern you created in step 6, and click OK.

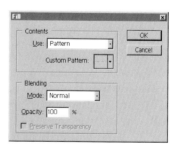

9. Check the overall pattern for texture and color balance. If you are satisfied with the test, the pattern is ready to use. To apply the pattern to an image, close the test file and continue with step 10.

If the pattern isn't tiling correctly, test the original tile in Illustrator to ensure that it tiled correctly there. Fix the problem and repeat steps 1 through 8.

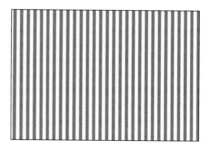

10. Open the file to which you will add the pattern.

In this example, the image was created using the Poster Edges & Smart Blur filter combination shown on page 196.

11. Create a new layer above all the current layers where you will add the pattern. Name the layer Pattern.

12. Select the area you want to fill with the pattern. With the Pattern layer still active, click the Add Layer Mask button at the bottom of the Layers palette to create a layer mask from the selection.

13. Click the Pattern layer thumbnail in the Layers palette to select the image and deselect the layer mask. Choose Edit > Fill to fill the layer with the pattern.

14. Adjust the layer blending mode if necessary, and add layer effects if desired. Save the file.

In this example, the Pattern layer mode was set to Difference and an inner shadow layer effect was added to give the stripes a bit of dimension.

Marbled paper

Adobe Photoshop 7.0 or later

The Italian art of marbleizing is difficult and messy, but it produces some really lovely papers and fabrics. Now that Photoshop has the Liquify filter, you can make your own digital marbled paper without the oily paints. To get the base colors, you'll select a tiny area of any digital image. Then you'll enlarge it, blur it, and liquify it. Once you've created several sheets of marbled paper, put them to use in a collage or as backgrounds for pages in a book.

1. Open an RGB image that contains the colors you want to use in your marbling.

This example is part of a larger photograph of two women in jeans and T-shirts, sitting on the grass.

2. Use the zoom tool to zoom in on the image until you can see the individual pixels. Use the rectangular marquee tool to select an area that contains the colors you want to use.

In this example, the dark jeans and a bit of the green shirt were selected.

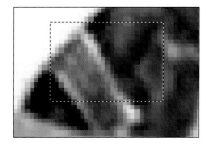

3. Choose Edit > Copy to copy the selection. Open a new RGB file. It should be several times larger than the selection you just copied. Choose Edit > Paste. The small selection will be pasted on a layer of its own called Layer 1.

4. Choose Photoshop > Preferences > General (OS X) or Edit > Preferences > General (Mac OS and Windows). Change the Interpolation to Nearest Neighbor. Click OK.

Nearest Neighbor keeps the pixel colors from blurring together when you scale them. You'll scale them in the next step.

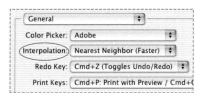

5. Choose Edit > Free Transform. Enlarge the selection to the size of the file. Press Return/Enter to complete the transformation.

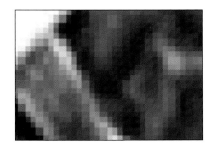

6. Choose Filter > Blur > Gaussian Blur. Enter a small number just to soften the hard edges of the pixels. It will vary according to your file size and resolution.

This example of a 300-ppi image used a blur radius of 1.2.

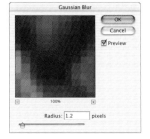

7. Choose Filter > Liquify. In the Liquify dialog box, select the warp tool and set the brush size. Use a brush that has a diameter roughly the size of two of the color squares in your image. If you're not sure how big to make it, move the pointer over the image to compare the brush size to the squares.

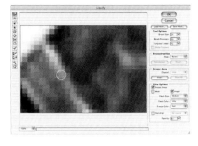

8. Using the warp tool, make strokes across the image. Keep the strokes close to each other and try alternating the direction. Don't scribble back and forth; make one gentle stroke in one direction and then make another stroke right next to it in the opposite direction. If you want to swirl the colors, make the curved strokes with large, slow motions.

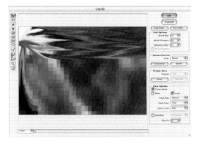

9. Once you have finished warping the image and are satisfied with the result, click OK.

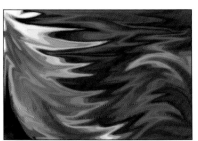

10. If you want to adjust the colors or saturation of the marbled paper, choose Image > Adjustments > Hue/Saturation. Turn on the Preview option, and make your changes. If you want to place your marbled paper inside of a shape, continue with the next step.

In this example, the Hue was changed to a greener color and the Saturation was increased.

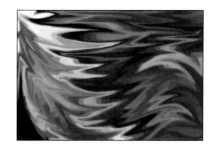

Colorizing marbled paper

1. Duplicate Layer 1 to retain a copy of the original marble.

2. Choose Image > Adjustments > Hue/Saturation. Turn on the Preview option, and experiment with the Hue, Saturation, and Lightness values until you are satisfied with the result. Click OK.

3. Repeat the entire technique or just steps 1 and 2 of the Colorizing Marbled Paper technique until you have as many colored marble papers as you need.

4. To use the marbled paper in an illustration like this example, follow steps 8 through 14 of the "Painted Paper Illustrations" technique on page 4.

Don't forget to return your Interpolation preferences (step 4 on page 117) to Bicubic when you've finished with this technique.

Textured 3-D graphics

Adobe Photoshop 7.0 or later
Adobe Illustrator 10 or later

Use the Overlay mode in the Layers palette of Photoshop to easily add photographic or painterly textures to three-dimensional grayscale graphics created in Illustrator. Simply place the graphic on a layer in Photoshop. You then copy a texture onto an adjacent layer and combine the two layers using the Overlay mode. If you have several shapes to texturize, it's recommended that you create a separate file for each shape and then combine them in another file using flattened versions of the final texturized graphic. Don't be intimidated by the length of this technique. It's really very easy!

1. Before you copy and paste paths from Illustrator to Photoshop, adjust Illustrator's preferences. Choose Illustrator > Preferences > Files & Clipboard (OS X) or Edit > Preferences > Files & Clipboard (Mac OS or Windows). Select the AICB option and click the Preserve Paths option.

2. Create a three-dimensional shape in Illustrator. Paint the shape with shades of gray only. Do not use 100% black or white. Scale the artwork, if necessary, to its final size. Select all of the shapes and choose Edit > Copy to copy them to the Clipboard. Save the file.

You can create this graphic with the Photoshop shape tools, but it's easier in Illustrator.

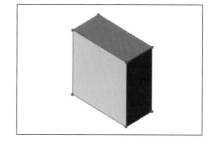

3. Create a new RGB file in Photoshop at the size and resolution you want for the final image. Choose Edit > Paste and select the Paste As Path option. Click OK. Do not move the path from its pasted position.

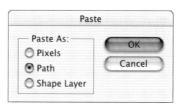

4. Double-click the Work Path name in the Paths palette to open the Save Path dialog box, and rename the path 3D Outline. Click in the blank area of the palette to deselect the path.

You will use this path several times in later steps to select the outlines of the different surfaces of your object.

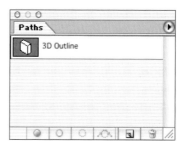

5. Choose File > Place, select the Illustrator file you created in step 1, and click Place. Do not move or scale the object, to ensure that it aligns perfectly with the paths you pasted in step 3. Press Return/Enter to rasterize the image.

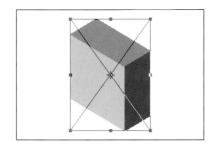

6. Select the new layer that was created by placing the graphic in step 5, and double-click its name. Rename the layer 3D Base.

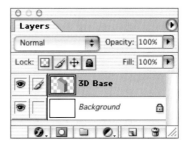

7. Open a file with the texture that you want to appear on the surface of the three-dimensional shape. Select the area of the texture that you want to use. Use the move tool to drag the selection from its window into the 3D Base file window.

8. Using the Layers palette, name the new layer Texture and change its blending mode to Overlay. Option/Alt-click between the Texture layer and the 3D Base layer to create a clipping group of the two layers.

You need a clipping group to prevent the Overlay mode from affecting other layers in your file.

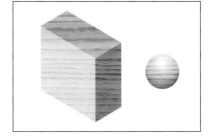

9. Evaluate the result. If your shape has only one visible plane, such as a cone or sphere, and you like the result, save the file. If your shape has angled sides that need adjusting, continue to the next technique, Creating Side Surfaces.

Areas filled with 50% black will show 100% of the texture. Areas filled with 100% black or white will show no texture.

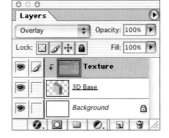

Creating side surfaces

1. Drag the 3D Base layer thumbnail onto the New Layer button at the bottom of the Layers palette to duplicate the layer. Then drag the Texture layer thumbnail to the New Layer button to duplicate that layer.

These duplicates will become the side panel. The duplicate Texture layer will be added to the layer group.

2. Move the 3D Base Copy layer up underneath the Texture Copy layer in the Layers palette. Option/Alt-click the line between the Texture layer and the 3D Base layer to re-create the clipping group. Rename the 3D Base Copy layer Side Base. Rename the Texture Copy layer Side Texture.

You should now have two separate, but identical, layer groups.

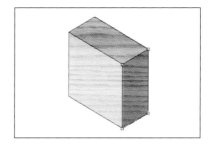

3. Activate the 3D Outline path in the Paths palette. Use the direct-selection tool to select the path that defines the side outline of your object.

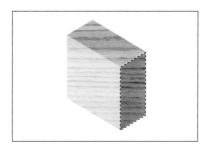

4. Click the Load Path as a Selection button at the bottom of the Paths palette to create a selection from the path. Turn off the path by clicking in the blank area of the Paths palette to make only the selection marquee active.

5. Select the Side Base layer and click the Add Layer Mask button at the bottom of the Layers palette.

The layer mask will mask out everything but the side area of the graphic.

6. Select the Side Texture layer and select the move tool. Then choose Edit > Free Transform. Transform the texture so that it fits naturally on the side plane of the object. Press Return/Enter to complete the transformation.

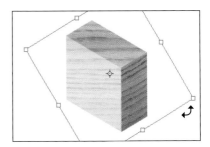

In this example, the wood grain was rotated so that it aligned with the edge of the side, and was scaled a bit.

7. With the Side Texture layer still selected, use the move tool to reposition the texture layer. If you are satisfied with the result, save the file. If the top plane of the shape needs adjustment, continue to the next technique, Creating a Top Surface.

Creating a top surface

1. Repeat steps 1 and 2 of the Creating Side Surfaces technique to duplicate the 3D Base and Texture layers. Rename these layers Top Base and Top Texture.

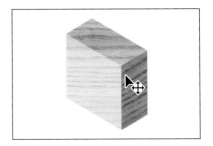

2. Turn on the 3D Outline path in the Paths palette. Use the direct-selection tool to select the path that defines the top outline of your object.

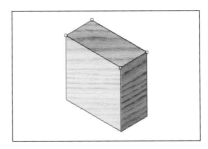

3. Click the Load Path as a Selection button at the bottom of the Paths palette to create a selection from the path. Turn off the path by clicking in the blank area of the Paths palette.

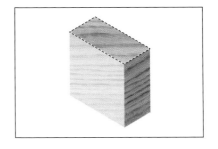

4. Select the Top Base layer and click the Add Layer Mask button at the bottom of the Layers palette.

The layer mask will mask out everything but the top area of the graphic.

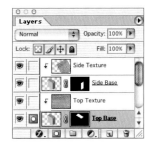

5. Select the Top Texture layer and select the move tool. Then choose Edit > Free Transform. Transform the texture so that it fits naturally on the top plane of the object.

Scaling the top texture horizontally makes it appear to recede.

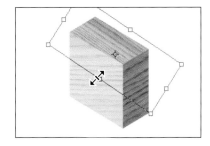

6. With the Top Texture layer still selected, use the move tool to reposition the texture layer. If you are satisfied with the result, save the file. If the front plane of the shape needs adjustment, continue to step 7.

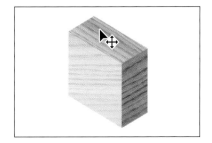

7. Repeat steps 2 through 6 to adjust the front plane of the object if desired. Use the Texture and 3D Base layers for the front planes. Repeat the entire technique for each three-dimensional shape you want to texturize.

4

Text Effects

Photos masked by type

Adobe Illustrator 10 or later
Or Adobe Photoshop 7.0 or later

You can create type masks for photographs in Illustrator or Photoshop. Type masks are easy to create and edit in both programs, thanks to layers and grouping. However, Illustrator generates PostScript language outlines whereas Photoshop generates rasterized type. You'll need to decide which kind of output you require. If you are printing the graphic, use Illustrator. If you intend the final graphic for a Web page, use the Photoshop technique. With both methods, heavy sans serif typefaces usually make the best-looking masks.

Illustrator versus Photoshop

Before you start, decide whether you want to use Illustrator or Photoshop to create the type. Use Illustrator if you want the clean, crisp edges that PostScript typefaces and printers can deliver. Compare the edge quality of the graphics at right. Both images are shown at the same resolution. The Illustrator outline is created from Bézier curves, and will always be smooth and sharp no matter what the printer or file resolution. The Photoshop edge is anti-aliased and slightly jaggy and fuzzy. If your graphic will be viewed on-screen and never printed or doesn't need special typographic adjustments, you can use Photoshop.

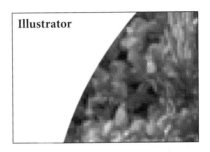
Illustrator

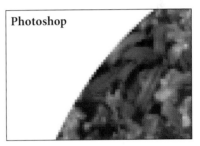
Photoshop

Illustrator method

1. Open or create a new file. Select the type tool, and create the type that will mask the image.

For optimal legibility of the type and image, use a large, bold typeface. A thin typeface design tends to lose its shape when filled with an image, and often the image within is unrecognizable.

2. With the type still selected, choose Window > Info to display the Info palette. Make a note of the width and height of the type to use in step 3.

These measurements will be helpful in determining the size your image needs to be. If it's too small, the type won't be completely filled.

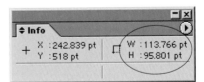

3. Switch to Photoshop and open the image you will mask with the type. Select the crop tool in the toolbox. Refer to the numbers you noted in step 2 and, in the Options bar, enter a width and height value that is almost a quarter larger than the width and height of the type. Enter whatever resolution you want.

4. Use the crop tool to select the area of the image that will be masked by type. Press Return/Enter to crop the image. Save the file.

It's a good idea to keep the image about 20% larger than the type. That way you'll have room to reposition the image within the type once it's masked.

5. Return to the Illustrator file and choose File > Place. Navigate to the Photoshop file you saved in step 4, and click Place. While the image is still selected, choose Object > Arrange > Send to Back to move the image behind the type.

For the type to mask the image, it must be in front of the image.

6. Select both the type and the image, and choose Object > Clipping Mask > Make. If this file will be combined with other graphics, it's a good idea to group the type mask with the image. To group the two, select both the type and image, and choose Object > Group. Save the file.

Photoshop method

1. Open the image that will be masked by type.

2. Select the type tool, and create the type that will mask the image.

For optimal legibility of the type and image, use a large, bold typeface. Thin typeface designs tend to lose their shape when filled with an image, and often the image within is unrecognizable.

3. Select the type layer in the Layers palette, and move it below the image layer. The type is now hidden by the image. Option/Alt-click the line between the type and image layers to create a layer group.

Even though the layers are now grouped, you can still edit the type or move the image around.

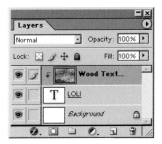

4. Once the image is positioned properly within the type, link the layers. This lets you move the two layers around without losing the relationship between them. Save the file.

Variation: Duplicate the image layer, and drag it down below the type layer so that the image layer isn't part of the layer group. Create a Hue/Saturation adjustment layer, and use the Colorize option to change the overall color of the image.

In this example, the image layer was inverted as well. To invert the image layer, select it, and choose Image > Adjustments > Invert.

Link the new background file and its adjustment layer to the type layer. Linking maintains perfect registration between the type and the background image if you move any of them.

In this example, a simple drop shadow was added to make the type stand out.

Embossed type

Adobe Photoshop 7.0 or later

The Layer Styles feature in Photoshop makes embossing type extremely easy and flexible. The first technique applies an emboss effect to type with the same color as the Background layer to make the type look as if it's really embossed on the background texture. Once you've embossed your type, you can give it the look and feel of gold metal with the second technique.

Embossed type

1. Open or create a file that will be the background surface for the embossed type. For best results, use a surface that contains texture. Select white as your foreground color. Select the type tool and enter your text.

2. With the type layer selected, click the Add Layer Style button at the bottom of the Layers palette. Use the pop-up menu to choose Bevel and Emboss in the Layer Style dialog box, and set the style to Inner Bevel. Don't click OK yet.

Don't worry about the other settings too much at this point. You may want to go back and adjust them at the end of the technique.

3. Click Blending Options in the Styles list on the left side of the Layer Style dialog box. In the Advanced Blending section, set the Fill Opacity to 10%.

Leaving just 10% white makes the type pop off the background a bit. You may want to adjust this percentage depending on the background.

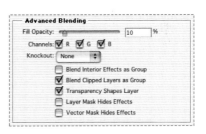

4. Click OK to view the results.

If the effect is too subtle, double-click the Layer Style icon on the type layer to reopen the Layer Style dialog box, and adjust the Fill Opacity. You can also exaggerate the effect by clicking Bevel and Emboss on the left side of the dialog box to redisplay the style's Structure options. Then increase the Size or Depth of the emboss.

Metallic gold embossed type

1. Create a file that will be the background surface for the gold type. For the most dramatic results, use a dark background. Create a gold foreground color of R = 249, G = 215, B = 121. Select the type tool and enter your text.

2. Command/Ctrl-click the type layer thumbnail in the Layers palette to create a selection of its transparency mask.

3. Choose Select > Save Selection to save it to a new alpha channel. Name the channel Type Mask.

4. Deselect. With the type layer still selected, click the Add Layer Style button in the Layers palette and choose Bevel and Emboss from the pop-up menu. Set the style to Inner Bevel and leave the settings at their default values.

5. Click the Type Mask channel in the Channels palette. Choose Filter > Blur > Gaussian Blur to soften the image.

This channel will be used in step 8 as a mask. More blur will produce a rounder, less beveled effect. Less blur will produce more defined bevels. This example used a radius of 3 pixels.

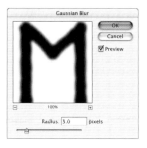

6. Click the RGB channel in the Channels palette, and then activate the type layer in the Layers palette.

Make any final copy changes. You'll apply a lighting effect that rasterizes the type and renders it no longer editable with the type tools.

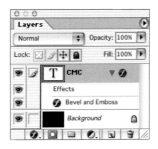

7. Choose Filter > Render > Lighting Effects. At the alert, click OK.

8. Select 2 o'clock Spotlight as the Style. Choose Type Mask as the Texture Channel. Deselect the White is High option to avoid making the type look debossed.

Lighting Effects comes with a set of predefined lighting styles that you may want to try. Use 2 o'clock Spotlight to ensure the results shown here.

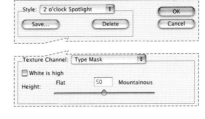

9. With the type layer still active, choose Filter > Artistic > Plastic Wrap. Use the following values: Highlight Strength = 11, Detail = 11, Smoothness = 15. Click OK.

The Plastic Wrap filter will add more highlights to make the type appear more metallic.

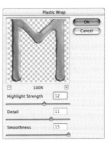

10. Choose Edit > Fade Plastic Wrap. Set the Mode to Hard Light to magnify the color, and click OK.

Corroded type

Adobe Photoshop 7.0 or later

I feel like flying
I long to be free
But Old Man Gravity
Is pullin' on me.

Some designers try to simulate an eroded or weathered type effect by making a series of photocopies in which each copy is made from the previous copy. The following technique lets you achieve a similar look with more control and less wasted paper. The basic technique produces a typeface with holes in it and corroded edges. The variation gives you a sketchy, scratchy look. A serif typeface design such as Times or Caslon will work well with the Corroded Type technique if you want the thin parts of the letters to look eaten away.

1. Create or open the file to which you want to add the corroded type.

2. Choose New Channel from the Channels palette menu. Select the Selected Areas option and name the channel Type. Click OK.

Channels are always grayscale, and they usually look like film negatives. In this technique, the channel looks like a positive grayscale image, and the areas of black and gray are the selection areas.

3. Press the D key to return the foreground and background colors to white and black. Then press the X key to reverse their positions. Use the type tool to create black type in the Type channel; then press Return/Enter. Use the move tool to position the type while it is selected.

Type created in channels becomes a selection, not an editable type layer.

4. While the type is still selected, choose Filter > Pixelate > Mezzotint. Choose Grainy Dots for the Type of mezzotint. Click OK.

The preview proxy may show the mezzotint affecting the white area as well as the type. But as long as the type is selected, the filter will apply only to the selected area.

5. Deselect the type and choose Filter > Brush Strokes > Spatter. Use the proxy preview to determine the values to use for Spray Radius and Smoothness. The amount will vary depending on the typeface, type size, and personal preference.

6. If you want to smooth out the holes a bit, choose Filter > Noise > Median. Turn on the Preview option, and select a Radius based on how smooth and rounded you want the type to be. Then click OK.

7. Save the file. The Type channel is now complete and ready to be used as a selection.

You'll use this selection in the next step to create the colored, corroded type.

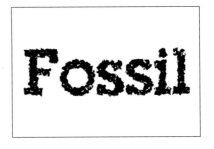

8. To add a color type layer to your artwork, open the Layers palette. Click the Background layer to view the composite color image again. Create a new layer and call it Corroded Type.

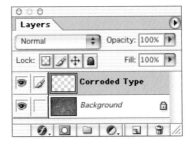

9. With the Corroded Type layer still selected, choose Select > Load Selection and load the Type channel as the selection.

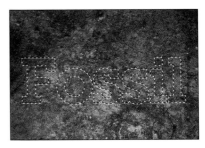

10. Select a foreground color as a fill for the type. Choose Edit > Fill and fill the selection with the foreground color. Save the file.

You can change the color later, without reloading the Type channel selection. Just turn on the Lock Transparent Pixels option in the Layers palette for the Corroded Type layer, and fill. Only nontransparent areas will fill with color.

Eroded type

1. Choose a typeface design that has varied thickness in the letterforms. Follow the first technique, except replace steps 4 through 6 with the following: Deselect the type. Choose Filter > Artistic > Palette Knife. Adjust the Softness, Stroke Size, and Stroke Detail until you have the desired amount of erosion.

2. Choose Filter > Sketch > Torn Edges. Start with the values shown at the right, and then adjust them for your typeface and size.

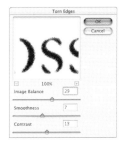

3. Continue with steps 7 through 10 of the preceding technique to complete the effect.

Variation: Follow the first technique except replace steps 4 through 6 with the following:

Deselect. Choose Filter > Brush Strokes > Sprayed Strokes. Use a Vertical Stroke Direction and start with a Stroke Length of 12 and a Spray Radius of 15. Adjust these values to your taste. For a really corroded look, reapply the filter with the same settings.

Type with multiple outlines

Adobe Illustrator 10 or later

You can create shapes with multiple outlines in Illustrator by using the Appearance palette to add strokes on top of each other and paint them with different colors and stroke weights. The top level in the Appearance palette is a color fill, which hides the half of the stroke that appears inside the path. Using this technique gives you the ability to edit the colors, line widths, and typeface easily. To use the appearance before you start with other images or on other objects, save it as a style. For help in determining line weights for the strokes, read the tip about stroking typefaces at the end of this technique.

1. Use the type tool to create the word or letters you want to outline.

For best results, avoid using script typefaces or specialty faces with inlines or other embellishments.

2. Choose Window > Type > Character, and enter a positive number for the Tracking value.

The amount needed varies with each typeface and the thickness of the thickest stroke. You can adjust the tracking and type style in step 11, when you've finished stroking the type.

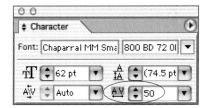

3. Choose Window > Appearance to display the Appearance palette. From the palette menu, choose Add New Fill.

Don't worry if the fill is the wrong color; you'll change that in the next step.

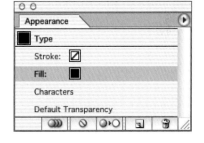

4. With the Fill item still selected in the Appearance palette, change the color in the Color palette, if desired.

5. With the type still selected, choose Add New Stroke from the Appearance palette menu.

You'll change the color and stroke weight in step 7.

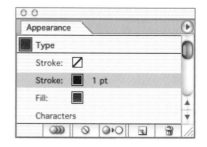

6. In the Appearance palette, drag the Stroke item down and place it beneath the Fill item.

The stacking order of strokes and fills directly affects an object's appearance. The Fill item should always be on top of the strokes to maintain the integrity of the original letterform. See the inset and illustrations at the end of this technique for more information.

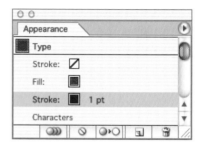

7. Evaluate the stroke weight and color. Change them if necessary. Remember that the stroke weight you use will effectively be cut in half in your illustration.

For example, a 1-point black stroke was used in this illustration; you see a 0.5-point stroke in the artwork because the top layer covers up the inner half of the stroke.

8. With the type still selected, choose Add New Stroke from the Appearance palette menu. Move the stroke down below the first stroke you made in the Appearance palette. Change its color in the Color palette. Make the stroke weight larger than the first stroke you made.

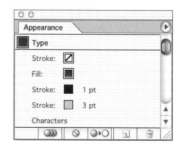

9. Repeat step 8 until you have as many strokes around the type as desired.

10. Click each Stroke item in the Appearance palette and in turn click the Round Join button in the Stroke palette.

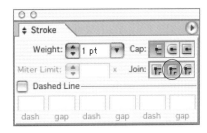

Depending on the typeface design you choose, the outlines may display some odd-looking corners. Using a Round Join for the stroke corners will correct this problem.

11. While the type is still selected, adjust the tracking if necessary. You can also change the typeface and type size if desired.

Remember that if you change the type size, the stroke weights will not change, so you may need to adjust them after resizing the type.

❧ *Stroking typefaces in Illustrator*

Before you begin, you'll probably want to determine the best stroke widths for your type outlines. When you stroke type, Illustrator creates the stroke from the center of the path that defines the outer edge of the letter. This means that a stroke value of 6 points will create a 3-point border outside the edge and a 3-point border inside it. The stroke value of each consecutive layer determines the width of the border beneath it; for example, a 4-point stroke on top of a 6-point stroke will produce a border of 1 point (6/2 – 4/2). You may want to do a little sketch like this one on the right before you start, so that you can figure out what stroke values to use.

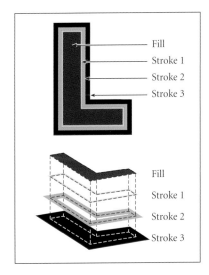

When stroking type, it's important to use the Appearance palette to layer the fill above the stroke. The fill above the stroke maintains the integrity and beauty of the original design. Notice how the heavy stroke eats away at the letterform in the letter that has the stroke above the fill.

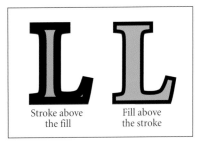

Stroke above   Fill above
the fill   the stroke

Rainbow scratchboard type

Adobe Photoshop 7.0 or later

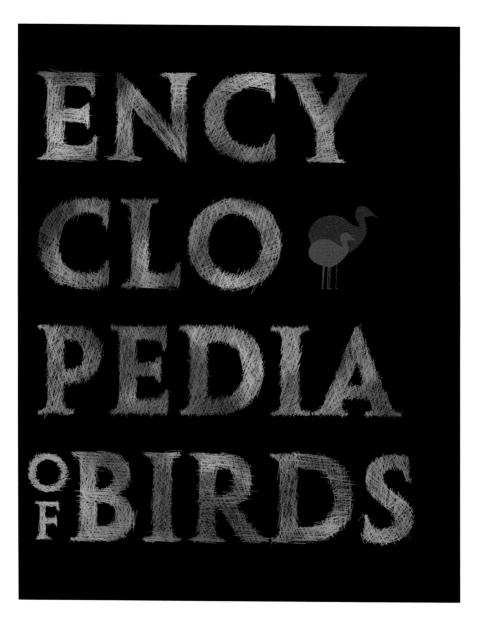

Remember when you were in grade school and you created artwork by scratching a design onto a painting covered with black wax crayon? This technique is the digital version of that style of illustration. First make a soft rainbow-colored paint layer. Then cover it with a black layer and proceed to scratch away a design. You can vary this method of using outlined type as a guide and use any outlined selection. If you want your drawing to be free-form, skip making a type outline layer. Be sure to use the History palette to take snapshots along the way so that you can undo mistakes without losing all of your work.

1. Create a new file. Select the gradient tool in the toolbox. Display the Gradient Editor dialog box by clicking the gradient swatch in the tool options bar. Select the Spectrum gradient and click OK. Then select the linear gradient tool in the tool options bar.

2. Drag the gradient tool across the width of the page to fill the entire file area with the Spectrum gradient.

3. Choose Filter > Distort > Ripple to smear the colors. Choose Large and set the Amount to 999%. Click OK.

4. Choose Filter > Distort > Twirl to mix the colors even more. Set the angle to 999°.

5. Choose Filter > Distort > Wave to distort the rainbow completely. Play with the Number of Generators option until you like the effect. Use Sine as the Type and select the Repeat Edge Pixels option. Click the Randomize button until the image is well distorted. Click OK.

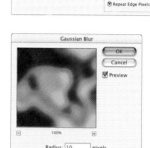

6. Choose Filter > Blur > Gaussian Blur to soften the colors and remove any sharp edges or abrupt color transitions. Adjust the Radius amount until no hard edges remain between colors.

7. Edit the rainbow image as needed so that it looks as if it were created with chalk pastels or watercolors.

8. Add a new layer and call it Black. Fill the layer with 100% black.

9. Add another new layer and call it Type Outlines.

This layer will contain an outlined version of the type you will use as a guide in step 15.

10. Select one of the type mask tools and use it to create a type selection.

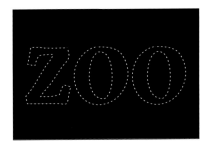

11. Select a bright yellow color in the Color palette. This example used a mix of R = 255, G = 255, B = 0.

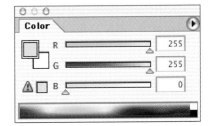

12. With the Type Outlines layer selected, choose Edit > Stroke. Stroke the type with 1 pixel and choose Outside as the location. Click OK, and deselect the type.

13. Select the eraser tool in the toolbox. In the tool options bar, set the Mode to Brush and the Opacity to 100%. Select a 1-pixel paintbrush in the Brushes palette.

These are good settings to start with, but you may want to experiment with other brushes and modes once you've mastered the technique.

14. Choose View > History or click its tab to display the History palette. Click the New Snapshot button to record the current state of the file.

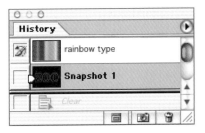

It's a good idea to take snapshots as you go along so that you can undo mistakes without having to completely redo the entire file each time.

15. Select the Black layer and begin scratching the black with the eraser tool using the type outlines as a guide. Hide and show the Type Outlines layer to view the results as you progress.

In this example, the whole letter was scratched in one direction.

16. Scratch the letterforms crosswise to give them more weight and a better defined shape.

17. Continue to scratch away the black until you are satisfied with the result. Hide the Type Outlines layer. When you are satisfied with the result, save the file.

Variation 1: Select the Black layer and click the Lock Transparent Pixels button in the Layers palette. Then fill the layer with another color.

In this example, the layer was filled with white.

Variation 2: Click the Background layer in the Layers palette. Click the New Adjustment Layer button at the bottom of the Layers palette. Choose Hue/Saturation. Turn on the Preview button and move the Hue, Saturation, or Lightness sliders until you are satisfied with the result.

In this example, the Hue slider was moved to +180.

Type on a circular path

Adobe Illustrator 10 or later

Is for cat,

CHICKEN, COW, COUGAR, CRAB, CAMEL, CRICKET, CATERPILLAR, COLT, COBRA, COCKATOO AND COYOTE

Illustrator does a wonderful job of setting type around a circle. But sometimes you want the type on the bottom of the circle to be positioned right side up instead of upside down. And sometimes you want the type to bend and stretch with the curve. The first technique shows you how to create type around a circle so that the type is always right side up. It also leaves the type undistorted. The second technique uses the Envelope distortion to place type on an arc in such a way that the type is stretched and distorted.

Undistorted circular type

1. Select the ellipse tool, press the Shift key, and create a circle that defines the inside baseline of your type.

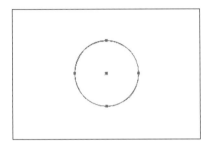

2. Select the path type tool and click the top anchor point of the circle. Enter only the text that you want to appear at the top of the circle. The text for the bottom of the circle will be entered in a later step.

All caps work better than upper- and lowercase letters because no ascenders or descenders bisect the arc that the letters form.

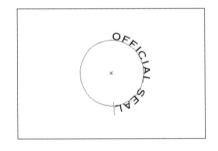

3. Choose Select > All to select the type you just entered. Choose Window > Type > Paragraph to display the Paragraph palette. Click the Align Center button to center the type across the top of the circle.

4. With the type still selected, choose the selection tool. Grab the top of the I-beam that appears in the center of the text and drag straight down, pressing the Shift + Option/Alt keys while dragging. When you get to the bottom point on the circle, release the mouse button and then the Shift + Option/Alt keys.

You've now made a copy of the type.

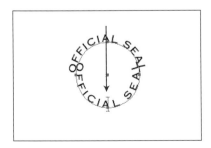

5. Select the path type tool, and choose Select > All to select the type you just duplicated on the bottom of the circle. Replace the type with the new text that you want to appear on the bottom half of the circle.

Don't worry if the type overlaps the top copy; you will adjust the point size later.

6. Choose Select > All to select all of the bottom type. Choose View > Type > Character to display the Character palette, and then choose Show Options from the palette menu. Click the Baseline Shift buttons in the Character palette to move the type so that the tops of the letters touch the edge of the circle.

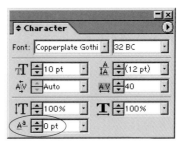

7. Depending on the type size and design, enter a fractional amount if necessary. In this example, the baseline shift is –6.5 points.

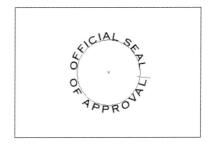

8. Choose the selection tool and select both circles with their type. Click the Font Size button to adjust the type size so that it fits around the circle.

You can also adjust the letterspacing to fit the letters around the circle. In this example, the tracking was set to 40.

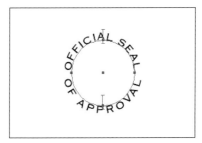

9. Adjust the position of the type on the circle if needed. Use the selection tool to drag the I-beam. Choose Illustrator > Preferences > Type & Auto Tracing (OS X) or Edit > Preferences > Type & Auto Tracing (Mac OS and Windows), and turn on the Type Area Select option to make the type easier to select.

In this example, the space between the two *L*'s was awkward, so it was reduced slightly.

10. To add a border, select the ellipse tool. Position the tool over the center point of the type circles. Option/Alt-drag from the center point outward. Press the Shift key to constrain the object to a circle. Release the mouse button and then the Shift + Option/Alt keys. Repeat this step for as many borders as you want.

Distorted type on a circle

1. Use the type tool to create the text that you want to appear on the top half of the circle.

2. Select the type with the selection tool. Choose Object > Envelope Distort > Make with Warp to open the Warp Options dialog box. Click the Preview button and use the settings shown in the illustration. Click OK.

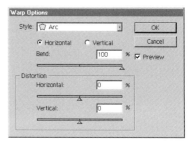

3. Choose Edit > Copy and then Edit > Paste in Front to create an exact duplicate of the type envelope. You'll edit the text in this copy in a few steps.

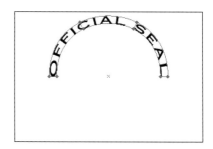

4. With the path still selected, choose Object > Envelope Distort > Reset with Warp. Click the Preview button and change the Bend value to –100%. Click OK.

Don't worry if the type arcs overlap each other. You'll fix that in the next steps.

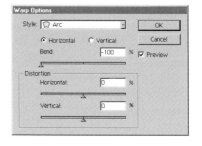

5. Use the View menu to turn on Smart Guides. Using the selection tool, grab the bottom arc by a top corner and move it until it snaps to the corner of the top arc.

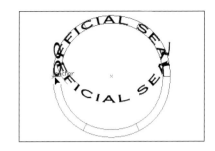

6. To edit the bottom text, choose Object > Envelope Distort > Edit Contents. Use the type tool to select the text, and enter the new text for the bottom of the circle.

7. If you want a space between the type on both circles, start and end the bottom type with a letter painted with no stroke and no fill. Just using a space won't work.

In this example, an *O* is placed at the beginning and end of the phrase "of approval." The *O*'s are filled and stroked with None.

8. If desired, add the borders, and you've finished. You can also change the color, typeface, and size of the type by following the instructions in step 6.

Recessed type

Adobe Photoshop 7.0 or later

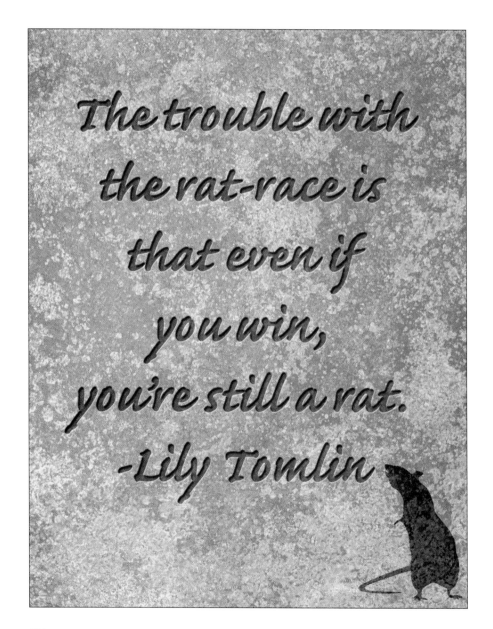

This technique makes your type look as if it were engraved into a surface. You can achieve a quick cutout effect by creating an Inner Shadow layer style for your type. But to make type really look carved out of the surface texture, you'll need to add two more layer styles. One style creates the beveled edge of the type cut out of the surface, and one style adds the surface texture back into the type recess. This technique works well with a variety of different typefaces, but try to stay away from styles with very thin stems. These fonts tend to fill in with shadow and don't look as good as those with a more evenly distributed thickness.

1. Open a file with a texture or background surface image out of which you will digitally carve type. Rename this layer Outer Texture.

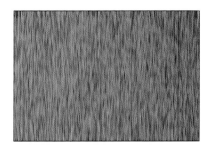

2. Change the foreground color to white and create the text.

If the background color is currently white, press the X key to switch the foreground and background colors.

3. Click the Add Layer Style button in the Layers palette, and choose Inner Shadow to add a cutout effect to the Type layer. Turn the Preview option on, and adjust the values for your particular typestyle and letter combination. Don't click OK yet.

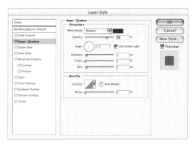

4. Click the words "Inner Glow" in the Styles list to select it and open its options. Click the color box and change the glow color to black. Change the Blend Mode to Multiply, and set the Opacity to 10%. Choose Center for the Source. With the Preview option turned on, adjust the Opacity level until you have a light gray letterform with a slight inner shadow. Click OK.

5. Use the move tool to adjust the position of the type against the background. The type will remain editable. However, you'll make a layer mask from a selection of the type in step 7; after that, you won't be able to move the type.

6. If you don't want the texture to show through the type, skip this step. Duplicate the texture layer, and call it Inner Texture. Move it beneath the Outer Texture layer.

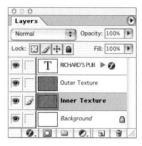

7. Command/Ctrl-click the type layer thumbnail to load a selection of its transparency mask. Choose Select > Inverse to select the transparent pixels on the type layer.

8. Click the Outer Texture layer in the Layers palette, and then click the Layer Mask button to create a mask.

Adding a layer mask creates edges of carved wood. In the next step, you'll add a layer style to bevel and highlight these edges.

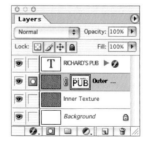

9. With the Outer Texture layer still active, click the Add Layer Style button in the Layers palette, and choose Bevel and Emboss. Select Inner Bevel as the Style. Turn on the Preview option and adjust the values for your typestyle and letter combination.

You'll see the edges of the texture grow in depth. This example used a yellow highlight instead of white for a softer effect.

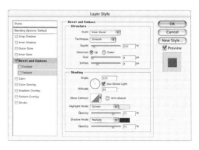

10. Evaluate the result. Adjust the layer style settings on the type or texture layer as desired. Some typestyles and sizes need more adjustment than others. Once you are satisfied with the effect, click OK.

11. Select the type layer, and change its layer blending mode to Multiply to reveal the texture on the Inner Texture layer.

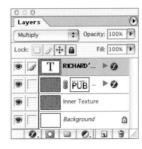

12. If you are satisfied with the effect, save the file. If desired, you can adjust the layer styles to change the size of the shadows, bevels, or highlights.

Variation 1: For a flat color inside the type, follow steps 1 through 10, but use a color instead of white as the foreground color in step 2.

Variation 2: For a colored texture inside the type, follow steps 1 through 12. Then select the Inner Texture layer. Create a Hue/Saturation adjustment layer and group it with the Inner Texture layer. Change the Hue, Saturation, and Lightness for the effect you want.

This example used these values:
Hue = –180, Saturation = –71, Lightness = –22.

1960s poster type

Adobe Illustrator 10 or later

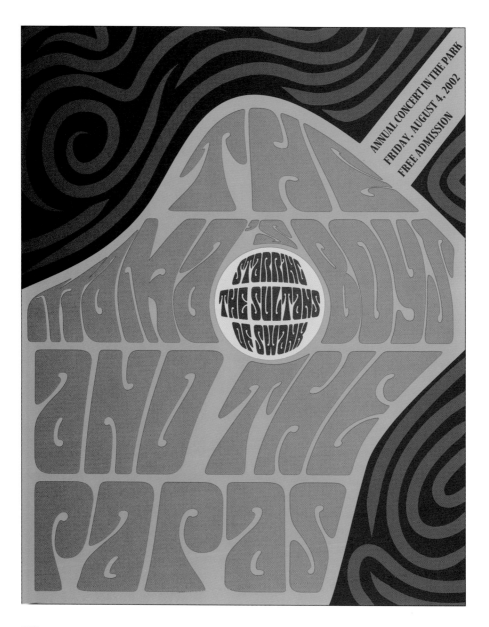

Many of the posters from the 1960s and '70s had hand-drawn typefaces that flowed into curved shapes. The posters were reminiscent of the Art Nouveau posters from the late 1800s. Inspired by flowers, leaves, and vines, the artists created sinuous shapes that encapsulated the type. With Illustrator's Envelope feature, you can create type just as they did in the '60s. First you create the basic shape and divide it into type containers. Then you create the type and combine it with the shape to distort it. Choose your typeface carefully. The ones that work best are very fat, dense display faces.

1. In a new Illustrator file or on a new layer, create the basic shape that will contain all of your type.

Keep the shape as simple as possible. The more intricate and complicated the shape, the less predictable (and satisfactory) the type distortion will be.

2. In the Layers palette, name the layer that contains the shape Type Background. Choose Duplicate "Type Background" from the Layers palette menu. Rename the new layer Type Shapes. Hide the Type Background layer.

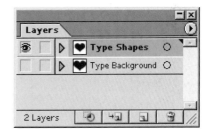

3. Using the pen tool, create lines that define where the type shapes will separate. Paint the lines with a stroke weight that's the width of space that you want between each type shape.

In this example, the lines are 2-pt strokes because the desired separation between the type blocks is 2 points.

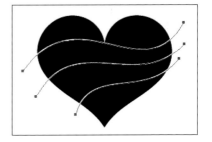

4. Select all of the lines you created in step 3, and choose Object > Path > Outline Stroke. The lines have now become shapes. This will help when you create the separate type shapes in step 5.

If you want a backup file in case your type doesn't fit nicely and you need to change these lines, choose File > Save a Copy and save a backup version of the artwork at this stage.

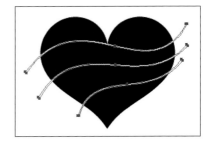

5. Display the Pathfinder palette. With the selection tool, Shift-select the lines you just outlined and the basic shape. Option/Alt-click the Subtract button in the Pathfinder palette to subtract the lines from the basic shape at the same time you expand the lines into regular objects. While the artwork is still selected, choose Object > Ungroup. Deselect the art.

6. Use the type tool to create one type object for each shape. Choose a heavy, thick typeface. Plan the text according to the size of the shape that will hold the text.

For example, the two top shapes in the heart will contain small text blocks, while the two middle shapes will contain longer words or phrases.

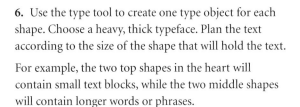

7. With the type still selected, choose Object > Arrange > Send to Back. Deselect the type.

8. Select one of the shapes, and then Shift-select the type object that will fit into it.

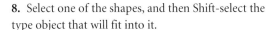

9. Choose Object > Envelope Distort > Make with Top Object.

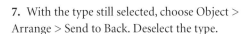

10. Repeat steps 8 and 9 for each type object in your artwork. If you are satisfied with the effect, skip to step 13. If you want to edit or change the type, continue with the next step.

If you want to edit the dividing lines and you saved a copy of the file at step 4, open that file; edit the lines and start again at step 5.

11. If you want to edit the text or change the typeface, select the envelope object that needs editing. Choose Object > Envelope Distort > Edit Contents. To view the type more easily, choose View > Outline. Select the type tool in the toolbox and make the type changes.

12. Choose View > Preview. If you are satisfied with the type changes, choose Object > Envelope Distort > Edit Envelope.

13. If you want to change the color of the type, select the envelopes and choose Object > Envelope Distort > Edit Contents. Use the Color palette to select a new fill color. Deselect the type.

14. To complete the effect, in the Layers palette show the Type Background layer. Select the original shape and paint it with a fill color. If you want the shape to appear slightly larger than the type, add a stroke to the shape that is the same color as its fill. Deselect and save the file.

Wet paint type

Adobe Photoshop 7.0 or later

Making your headline or logo look like it's a puddle of readable paint is really easy with this technique. Choose a typeface that has an interesting design with swashes, swirls, and plenty of variation in the width of the strokes. Script typefaces tend to look the best. Use the Plaster filter to give the type dimension and lighting, and then colorize it with an adjustment layer. The standard technique produces the type layer with its original transparency intact. If you want fatter type or eroded type, follow the variation instructions and merge the type with a background color.

1. Press the D key to set the foreground and background colors to black and white. Create a new file and fill the Background layer with 100% black.

2. Press the X key to switch white to the foreground color. Use the type tool to create the type that will become the wet paint type.

The best typefaces to use for this technique are script or calligraphic. If you want a slightly eroded look, choose a face with more pronounced thicks and thins.

3. Choose Layer > Rasterize > Type to convert the editable type into pixels on a transparent background.

To apply filters to type, you must first render type into pixels.

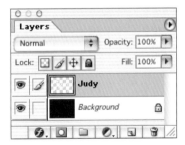

4. Use the brush tool to paint white drips and drops on the type layer.

Several brush sizes were combined to create the drips in this example. They won't look much like drips at this point, but they will turn into small blobs of paint later.

5. Duplicate the layer with the text and drips to keep a copy of its transparency mask for later use. Name the new layer Wet Paint.

6. With the foreground color still set to white and the Wet Paint layer selected, choose Filter > Sketch > Plaster. Start with the values shown here for Image Balance, Smoothness, and Light Direction. Adjust the values until you are happy with the preview, and then click OK.

7. Option/Alt-click the New Adjustment Layer button in the Layers palette. Select Hue/Saturation as the Type. Choose the Group With Previous Layer option in the New Layer dialog box so that the adjustment affects only the Wet Paint layer. Click OK to open the Hue/Saturation dialog box.

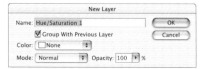

8. Select the Colorize option to apply color to the Wet Paint layer. Turn on the Preview option and adjust the Hue, Saturation, and Lightness sliders until you like the way the wet paint type looks. Click OK.

Colorize applies color to the image while retaining the highlight, midtone, and shadow values.

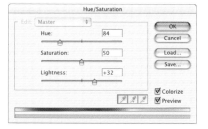

9. Evaluate the results with the current background. If you are satisfied, save the file. You can change the color by double-clicking the Hue/Saturation adjustment thumbnail in the Layers palette and altering the Hue value.

Notice that the Plaster filter maintains the original transparency mask so that the type is no thicker or thinner than it was in step 4.

Fat wet paint type

1. Follow steps 1 through 5 of the preceding technique. Then make a duplicate of the black Background layer. Move it up just beneath the Wet Paint layer.

2. Select the Wet Paint layer and choose Merge Down from the Layers palette menu.

A solid layer is required here because the Plaster filter needs a layer with no transparent pixels to be able to spread the type and make it look fatter (or thinner).

3. With the foreground color set to white and the Background Copy layer selected, choose Filter > Sketch > Plaster. Start with the values shown here for Image Balance and Smoothness. Adjust the values until you are happy with the preview, and then click OK.

To make the type even fatter, decrease the Image Balance or increase the Smoothness amount.

4. Continue with steps 7 through 9 of the preceding technique to complete the process.

The result will be a solid layer with white as the background. You can remove the white, if desired, by using the selection tools or Color Range command to select and delete the white. Be careful not to delete any white highlights that are within the letterforms.

Variation: For thinner or eroded looking type, follow the Fat Wet Paint Type technique, but use 46 for Image Balance and 6 for Smoothness with the Plaster filter.

Chrome type

Adobe Photoshop 7.0 or later

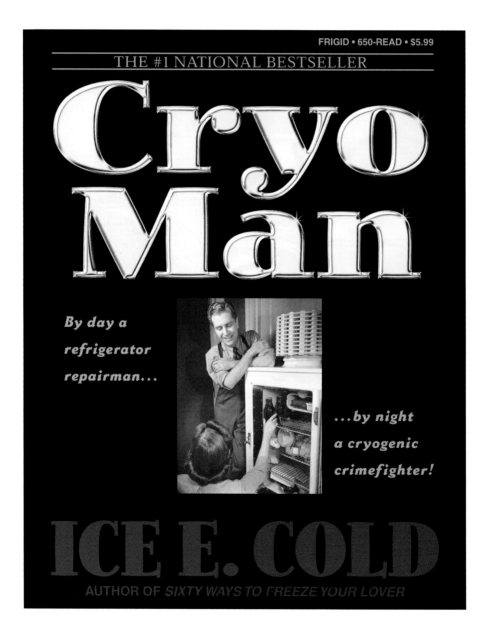

Chrome type can be created in Photoshop several ways, and most are fairly involved. You can do this technique in two stages. Steps 1 through 14 show you how to create embossed type that looks shiny and metallic to produce a gray type effect that can be colorized quickly with a Hue/Saturation adjustment layer. If you want to create the effect of the sky or another image reflecting off the type, continue with steps 15 through 24. Create your own sky using the Clouds filter or bring in another file with a sky for a different effect.

1. Create a new RGB file, and use the type tool to create the type that will become "chrome." Note the point size of the type, for use in step 5. Save the file.

2. Choose Layer > Rasterize > Type to change the layer into regular pixels.

Filters can't be used on type layers, so the layer must be rendered first. Once a type layer has been rendered, the type can be edited only as pixels, not as editable text.

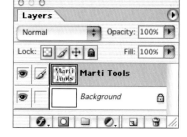

3. Command/Ctrl-click the type layer thumbnail to load a selection of the type.

4. Choose Select > Save Selection to create a new alpha channel. Name the channel Type, and click OK.

5. With the type still selected and its layer still active, choose Select > Feather. Enter a Feather Radius that is about 5% to 10% of the point size of your type. Note this number because you will use it again. Click OK.

In this example, the type was 48-point, so a 3-pixel feather was used.

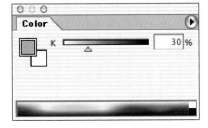

6. Display the Color palette and choose 30% black as the foreground color.

Choose Grayscale Slider from the Color palette menu to make this step easier.

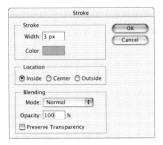

7. With the feathered selection still active, choose Edit > Stroke to add a soft gray stroke to the inside of the type. Enter the same value that you used in step 5. Select Inside as the Location. Click OK.

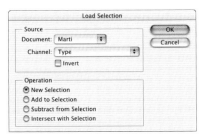

8. Choose Select > Load Selection, and select Type as the Channel. Click OK.

9. Choose Filter > Stylize > Emboss, and enter an angle of 135° and an amount of 160%. Experiment with the Height amount until you like the effect. Click OK.

10. Choose Select > Inverse to select the area around the type. Press Delete/Backspace to clean up some of the soft gray pixels that remain around the edges of the type.

11. Choose Select > Deselect to deselect.

12. Option/Alt-click the New Adjustment Layer button in the Layers palette to create a new adjustment layer. Select Curves as the Type, and choose the Group With Previous Layer option. Click OK.

13. Plot the following points on the Curves graph. The first number is the Input value, and the second number is the Output value.

A = 0, 255
B = 64, 31
C = 129, 238
D = 193, 63
E = 224, 255

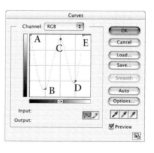

14. Click OK to apply the adjustment. Save the file, and stop here if you are satisfied with gray chrome type. To create a distorted reflection, continue with the next step.

If you want to color the type before stopping here, add a Hue/Saturation adjustment layer, select the Colorize option, and adjust the hue and saturation of the color effect.

Adding a sky reflection

1. Choose Window > Channels to display the Channels palette. Option/Alt-drag the Type channel onto the New Channel button to duplicate it. Name the copy Blurred Type. Click OK.

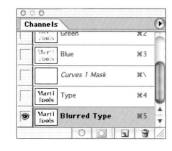

2. Choose Filter > Blur > Gaussian Blur. Blur the type quite a bit, using this example as a guide. Your Radius amount will vary depending on the file resolution and type size. Click OK.

3. Choose Duplicate Channel from the Channels palette menu. Select New as the Document and name the new file Blurred Type Map. Click OK. Save the Blurred Type Map file and close it.

You will use this file with the Glass filter in step 7, so remember where you saved it.

4. Click any layer in the Layers palette to reactivate the composite view of the type file. Option/Alt-click the New Layer button and name the new layer Sky.

5. Select RGB Sliders from the Color palette menu. Choose white as the background color and blue as the foreground color. Use the blue mix that is shown here or adjust it to your own taste.

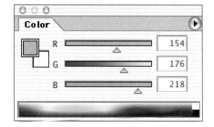

6. Choose Filter > Render > Clouds. To get more contrasting clouds, hold down the Option/Alt key as you choose the Clouds filter. Repeat this step until you have a cloudy sky that you like.

Each time you run the Clouds filter, the results will be different.

7. Choose Filter > Distort > Glass. Choose the Load Texture option from the Texture pop-up menu. Navigate to the Blurred Type Map file that you saved in step 3 and click Open. Use a Distortion of 20 and a Smoothness of 10. Click OK.

8. Set the Sky layer mode to Darken. Then Option/Alt-click on the line between it and the Curves layer to add it to the type layer group. If you are happy with the results, save the file. To fine-tune the contrast, continue with the next step.

9. Double-click the Curves adjustment layer icon to open the Curves dialog box. Adjust the points on the graph until you are happy with the contrast. Click OK.

This step lets you change the thickness of the dark reflections around the edges of the type.

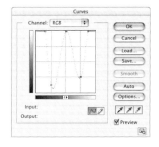

10. Save the file.

5 Special Effects

Simulated film grain

Adobe Photoshop 7.0 or later

Fine-textured grain technique (72 ppi)

Fine-textured grain technique (300 ppi)

Colored grain technique (72 ppi)

Colored grain technique (300 ppi)

Graininess is a mottled texture created by clumps of silver on photographic film. This quality is usually seen in greatly enlarged photographs or in photographs shot with a fast film speed. This section has four techniques for adding grain to your image. Refer to the examples below to see which will work best for your image. It's recommended that you use images that have a soft, ethereal quality or subject matter for this technique. You will end up with a softer, slightly impressionistic or misty image. All filter values used in these examples are the same values used in the technique.

Clumpy grain technique (72 ppi)

Clumpy grain technique (300 ppi)

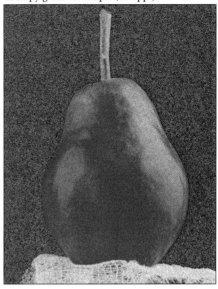

Impressionistic grain technique (72 ppi)

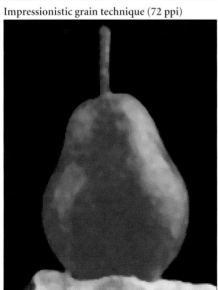

Impressionistic grain technique (300 ppi)

Fine-textured graininess

1. Open the file to which you will add grain. Choose Filter > Noise > Add Noise. Select the Monochromatic option so that only the texture changes and not the color. Enter the desired noise amount. Click OK.

2. Evaluate the result and save the file.

Sometimes the fine-textured grain is quite subtle on a high-resolution file. For a more pronounced effect, increase the amount of noise or try one of the following techniques.

Colored film grain

1. Open an RGB file and choose Filter > Texture > Grain. Select the Enlarged grain type. Experiment with the Intensity and Contrast values until you are happy with the proxy preview. Click OK.

2. Evaluate the result and save the file.

This variation adds new colors to your image. You will see hints of pure Red, Green, and Blue values sprinkled throughout the image.

Clumpy film grain

1. Open an RGB file and choose Filter > Artistic > Film Grain. Start with the values used here and adjust them for your image. Click OK.

2. Choose Filter > Noise > Median. Set the Radius to 1 pixel.

The Median filter will soften the grain and make it clumpy.

3. Evaluate the result and save the file.

This is a good technique to use when you want to simulate the way real photographic grain looks on a greatly enlarged image.

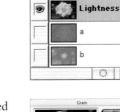

Impressionistic grain

1. Open your file and choose Image > Mode > Lab Color. Select the Lightness channel in the Channels palette.

The Lightness channel controls the color values in the image but not the hues.

2. Choose Filter > Texture > Grain. Select the Clumped grain type. Start with the values shown here for Intensity and Contrast, and then adjust them for your image. Click OK.

3. Return to the Lab channel to evaluate the result. Save the file.

The resulting image is the softest and most impressionistic of all of the variations shown. Choose this method when you want the photograph to have a painterly quality, but retain enough detail to look photographic.

Posterized photographs

Adobe Photoshop 7.0 or later

Using the Posterize command to posterize color images can produce some unexpected results because Photoshop posterizes each channel of a color image. A two-level posterization, for example, produces two colors in each channel of an image, generating a total of eight colors in an RGB image (2 x 2 x 2). This technique gives you more control over the colors and the number of colors themselves (by converting the image to grayscale first). This technique lends itself well to process or custom color inks.

1. Open the image that you want to posterize.

2. Duplicate the Background layer and call the new layer Smart Blur.

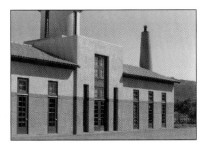

3. Choose Image > Adjustments > Channel Mixer to remove the color from the Smart Blur layer. Select the Monochrome option. Turn on the Preview option and move the color sliders until you have good contrast and definition of the important shapes in your image.

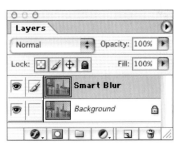

4. Choose Filter > Blur > Smart Blur to remove the detail and flatten out the gradations. Start with the Radius and Threshold values shown here, and then adjust them for your image. Set the Quality to High and the mode to Normal.

The goal here is to remove most of the texture and end up with flat shapes.

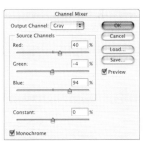

5. Duplicate the Smart Blur layer and name it Posterized. You will now posterize this layer.

Save the Smart Blur layer intact because you can experiment with different layer modes at the end of the technique.

6. Choose Image > Adjustments > Posterize. Turn on the Preview button so that you can see the effect.

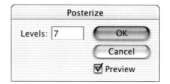

7. Select the number of levels of posterization. Try different numbers to see what detail is lost or retained. The goal is to simplify the image into large flat shapes without losing critical detail. When you find the correct level, click OK.

In this example, 7 levels were used.

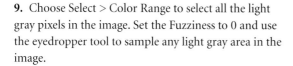

8. Identify areas of unwanted detail, and then select and fill them with the desired shades of gray. You can use the brush tool to cover unwanted areas as well. Continue with this process until you are ready to add the color.

In this example, the white areas on the face of the building were filled in.

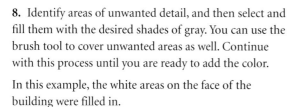

9. Choose Select > Color Range to select all the light gray pixels in the image. Set the Fuzziness to 0 and use the eyedropper tool to sample any light gray area in the image.

In this example, the light gray that defines the face of the building was sampled. Color Range selects all the pixels of that value.

10. Use the Color palette to select the color that you want to use in place of the gray, and fill the selection with it.

For more predictable results, try to match the tonal value of the color to that of the selected gray value.

11. Repeat steps 9 and 10 to select a second shade of gray and change its color throughout the picture.

12. Repeat steps 9 and 10 until all the shapes are filled with a color. Use the pencil or brush tool to retouch areas that are distracting.

In this example, the bits of texture in the foreground area were painted over.

Variation: If you want an image that is a variation of tones made from one color, skip steps 9 through 12. Option/Alt-click the New Fill layer button in the Layers palette and drag up to select Solid Color. Select the Group With Previous Layer option and change the Mode to Overlay. Click OK.

When the Color Picker appears, move it away from your image so that you can see the results as you sample different colors. When you're satisfied with the color effect, click OK.

Blended image layers

Adobe Photoshop 7.0 or later

Photoshop offers many, many ways to blend images together. Here are three different ways using layer masks, layer styles, and layer groups. Each one creates a different effect. The easiest to learn and use is the layer mask blending. Create a gradient layer mask to blend smoothly from one layer to another. If you're a more adventurous user, try playing with the layer styles blending. The effects you get will depend on the images you start with and their highlight and shadow values. And if you want to mask several layers at once without having to flatten them, use the layer group technique.

Layer Mask Blending method

1. Open or create an image file.

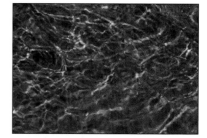

2. Open another file and select the move tool. Position the image windows so that you can see both of them on-screen at once. Use the move tool to drag and drop the image of one file onto the other, pressing the Shift key before you release the mouse button to center the layer on top of the other layer.

3. With the new layer still selected, click the Add Layer Mask button in the Layers palette. Press the D key to return the foreground and background colors to black and white.

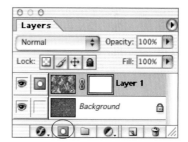

4. Select one of the gradient tools. Click the area to the right of the gradient swatch to display the pop-up gradient palette, and choose the foreground to background gradient from the gradient palette. Draw a gradient on the layer mask. The white areas of the gradient will reveal the top layer, and the black areas will reveal the layer underneath.

Try different gradients and angles for different effects.

Layer Options Blending method

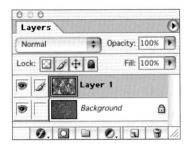

1. Follow steps 1 and 2 of the Layer Mask Blending technique.

2. Double-click the layer thumbnail of the upper layer in the Layers palette to open the Layer Style dialog box. To drop out the darkest areas of the top layer, move the black shadow triangle on the This Layer slider to the right.

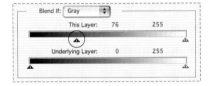

All pixel values that fall into this range will disappear from view and reveal the layer underneath.

3. To soften the transition from layer to layer, split the shadow triangle by holding down the Option/Alt key and dragging one side away from the other. You will see two half triangles. When you like the effect, click OK.

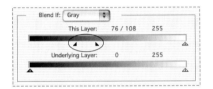

The lower layer is now revealed through the darkest areas of the upper layer.

4. If desired, edit and re-edit by double-clicking the layer to display the Layer Style dialog box and making additional adjustments.

5. To reveal the lower layer in the highlight areas of the upper layer, open the Layer Style dialog box again. Set the shadow slider back to 0. Move the white highlight triangle on the This Layer slider to the left. Option/Alt-drag it to split it for a smoother image transition.

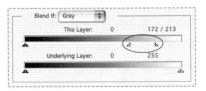

6. When you are satisfied with the preview, click OK.

The result shows that the lower image is revealed through the lightest values of the upper image.

7. Change the layer blending mode of the upper layer for other blending effects.

In this example, the layer blending mode was set to Difference with the Layer Options set to the values used in step 5. The water texture shows through in the darker areas, and the water image shows in the lighter areas resulting in a batik-like effect.

Layer Group Blending method

1. Open a file that has two or more layers. One of the layers should have a silhouette or shape that you want to use as a mask for one or more of the other layers. Position it below the layers it will mask.

This example uses two butterflies.

2. Option/Alt-click the line in between each of the layers you want to group. The thumbnail becomes indented, and the base layer name is underlined to remind you that it is the mask for the layers above it.

Once the layers are grouped with that base layer, the other layers adopt the transparency mask of the base layer.

In this example, the two layers that make the batik image created in the preceding step 7 are masked by the two butterflies. The background image is now the lowest layer and is not part of the Layer group.

Scanned objects as masks

Adobe Photoshop 7.0 or later

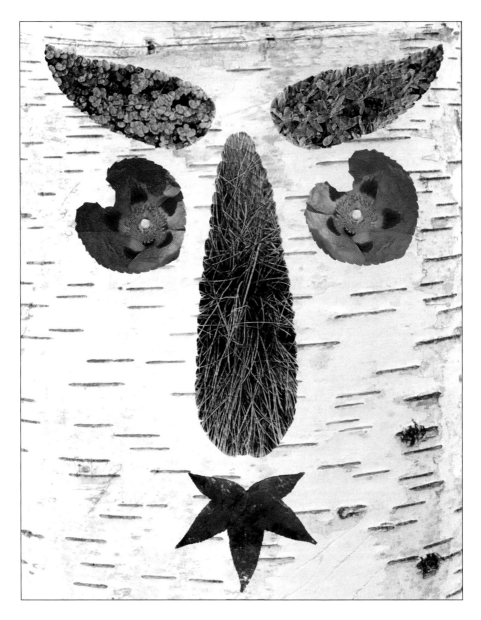

Photoshop features lots of ways to do many things—and masking images is no exception. In this technique, you'll learn two different ways to mask an image with another scanned image. In both methods, you create a silhouette from the scanned image and use it as the mask shape. Use the Clipping Group method if you want to experiment with layer modes and transparency. Not only can the scanned image be used as a mask, but its color and texture can also be integrated into the final effect. Use the Layer Mask method if you want to play with gradient blends between the image and its mask.

Clipping Group method

1. Using a white background, scan the object from which you want to create the mask.

Use a white background so that selecting it will be easy in step 3.

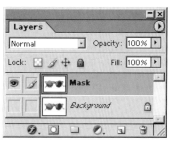

2. Preserve the original image by duplicating its layer. Name the layer Mask. Hide the original layer.

3. Choose Select > Color Range to select the white background around the object. Position the eyedropper tool over the white background and click. Use the other eyedropper tools to get a good mask of the entire white background. Click OK.

The only areas that should be selected are the ones that will not be part of the final mask.

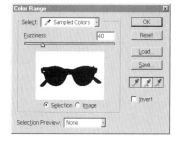

4. If the mask shape contains selected areas, deselect them now. Once you have everything outside of the mask shape selected, press Delete/Backspace to remove the pixels.

5. Deselect. Create a new layer with the image that will be masked and name it Image.

You can bring layers in from other files by copying and pasting, duplicating layers, or dragging and dropping.

6. Option/Alt-click the line between the two layers in the Layers palette to group them.

The bottom layer in a clipping group acts as a mask for all other layers within the group. Transparent areas will block out the image above, and the area that contains pixels will display the upper layers.

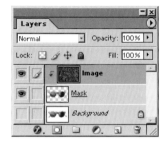

7. Select the move tool in the toolbox, and adjust the way the image falls within the mask. Make the Image layer active, and move it around until you are satisfied with the effect. Save the file.

Add a filled layer and place it beneath the Mask and Image layers, if desired.

Layer Mask method

1. Follow steps 1 through 5 of the Clipping Group method. Command/Ctrl-click the Mask layer thumbnail to load its shape as a selection.

2. Select the Image layer in the Layers palette. Click the Add Layer Mask button at the bottom of the Layers palette to create a layer mask.

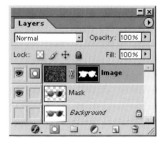

3. Click the link icon between the layer mask thumbnail and the Image layer thumbnail to unlink the two. Click the Image thumbnail.

Layer masks are linked to their layer image by default. Unlinking them lets you move them independently.

4. Use the move tool to adjust the positioning of the image within the layer mask. When you are satisfied with their relationship, relink them by clicking between their thumbnails in the Layers palette.

Keep the layer linked with its mask so that you can move the two as a group.

Variation 1: To maintain some of the texture and color of the Mask layer image, click the Image layer and change the blending mode.

In this example, the blending mode was set to Overlay.

Variation 2: Complete the Layer Mask method. Then load the Mask layer as a selection by Command/Ctrl-clicking its thumbnail in the Layers palette. Click the layer mask thumbnail of the Image layer.

Only the selected area of the layer mask will be affected in the next step.

Select the gradient tool and create a gradient within the selection. When you are satisfied with the effect, deselect and save.

The gradient on the layer mask creates a smooth blend between the image on the Mask layer and the image on the Image layer.

Reverse shapes

Adobe Illustrator 10 or later

Overlapping type and graphics is a hallmark of Art Deco graphic design. You can use these techniques, however, for any overlapping shapes whose colors you want to change at the point where the shapes overlap. If you want to be able to move the shapes after creating the reversed effect, use the Compound Path technique. If you want to paint shapes with different colors, use the Pathfinder technique.

Compound Path technique

1. Create the background element of your design.

Keep in mind that the paint attributes of the backmost object will be adopted by the other objects in the compound path.

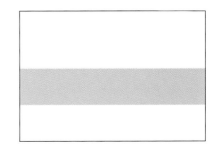

2. Create the objects or type that will reverse out of the background element. Position them as you want them in the final design.

3. If you are not using type as an element, skip this step. If you are using type, select it and choose Type > Create Outlines.

4. Select the background element and the foreground type or elements. Choose Object > Compound Path > Make.

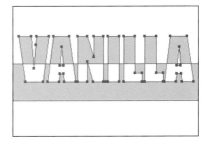

5. Deselect everything and check your work. Place an element behind the compound path, and notice that you can see through the "holes" that were created in the background element of the compound shape.

In this example, a black drop shape was placed behind the compound path.

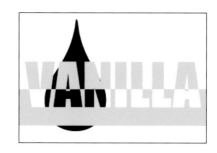

6. Use the group-selection tool to adjust elements of the compound path. To select an element, click its edge. To select a compound element, like the *A* in the illustration, click the edge of the element twice with the group-selection tool.

You can move, reshape, or transform the objects within the compound path. Changing an object's color, however, updates the entire compound path.

Pathfinder technique

1. Create the background element of your design.

The paint attributes of this object will change to that of the topmost object after you use the Pathfinder command in step 4.

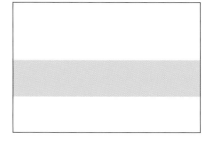

2. Create the objects or type that will reverse out of the background element. Position them as you want them in relation to the background element; after step 4, you won't be able to readjust the position of the elements.

3. If you are not using type as an element, skip this step. If you are using type, select it and choose Type > Create Outlines.

4. Select the background element and the foreground type or elements. Choose Window > Pathfinder to display the Pathfinder palette. Option/Alt-click the Exclude button.

Using Option/Alt with the Exclude button expands the artwork at the same time. Not expanding the artwork when using the Pathfinder palette creates only a compound path.

5. Use the direct-selection tool to select the objects you want to repaint, and change them as desired.

Each remaining area of color is now a separate object, and you no longer can move the original artwork elements. The overlapping areas that look white are actually "holes" in the artwork.

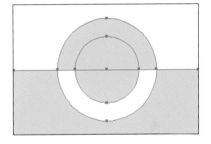

Correcting compound path problems

Some objects that you wanted to be transparent may be solid, or vice versa. Usually these objects were already compound paths before you compounded them again. To correct this problem, you must reverse the direction of these paths.

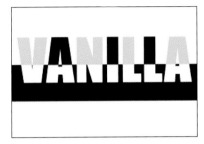

Use the direct-selection tool and select one of the paths that isn't reversing properly. Choose Window > Attributes. Click the Reverse Path Direction button that is not selected. Continue selecting paths and changing directions until the artwork is displayed correctly.

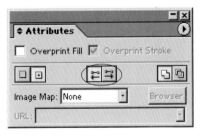

In this example, the path direction of the inner circle needed changing before it would display properly.

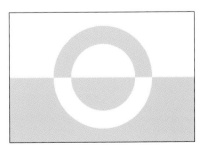

Filter combinations

Adobe Photoshop 7.0 or later

Original 150-ppi RGB images.

Blur & Diffuse

1. Choose Filter > Blur > Gaussian Blur.
Use a Radius of 2 pixels.

2. Choose Filter > Stylize > Diffuse. Use Normal
mode and apply the filter three more times.

Mosaic & Ripple

1. Choose Filter > Pixelate > Mosaic.
Use a Cell size of 10.

2. Choose Filter > Distort > Ripple.
Use Medium size at 100%.

Pointillize & Facet

1. Choose Filter > Pixelate > Pointillize.
Use a Cell size of 5.

2. Choose Filter > Pixelate > Facet. Apply the filter
two more times.

Sometimes you want a texture or special effect that can't be achieved with the application of just one filter. Shown here are just a few of the hundreds of combinations that you can use to enhance images. Although the examples illustrate filters applied to the entire image, these combinations can also be applied to just a selected area. To create an effect shown here, apply the filters in the order indicated. Note, however, that the effect may vary with different image resolutions and modes. Use RGB images with these techniques because some of the filters won't work with CMYK images.

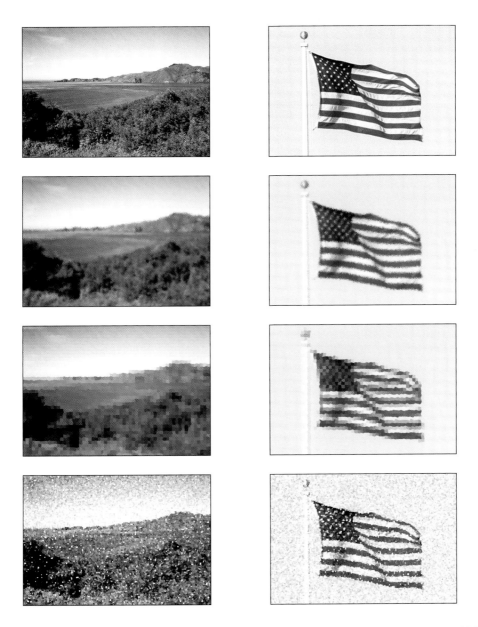

Pointillize & Glass

1. Choose Filter > Pixelate > Pointillize. Use a Cell size of 6.

2. Choose Filter > Distort > Glass. Use a Distortion of 1 and Smoothness of 2. Select Frosted as the Texture and leave the Scaling at 100%.

Find Edges & Crystallize

1. Choose Filter > Stylize > Find Edges.

2. Choose Filter > Pixelate > Crystallize. Use a Cell size of 6.

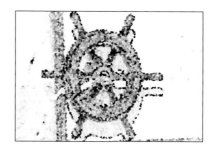

Poster Edges & Smart Blur

1. Choose Filter > Artistic > Poster Edges. Use an Edge Thickness of 4, an Edge Intensity of 2, and a Posterization of 3.

2. Choose Filter > Blur > Smart Blur. Use a Radius of 40 and a Threshold of 68. Set the Quality to High and the mode to Normal.

Graphic Pen & Palette Knife

1. Set the foreground color to Black. Choose Filter > Sketch > Graphic Pen. Set the Stroke Length to 15, Light/Dark Balance to 50, and Stroke Direction to Right Diagonal.

2. Choose Filter > Artistic > Palette Knife. Set the Stroke Size to 2, Stroke Detail to 3, and Softness to 1.

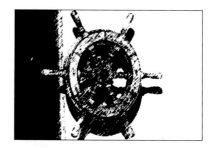

Dry Brush & Graphic Pen

1. Choose Filter > Artistic > Dry Brush. Set the Brush Size to 5, Brush Detail to 8, and Texture to 1.

2. Set the foreground color to Black. Choose Filter > Sketch > Graphic Pen. Set the Stroke Length to 15, Light/Dark Balance to 50, and Stroke Direction to Right Diagonal.

3. Choose Edit > Fade Graphic Pen. Set the mode to Soft Light at 100%.

Digital woodcuts

Adobe Photoshop 7.0 or later
Adobe Illustrator 10 or later

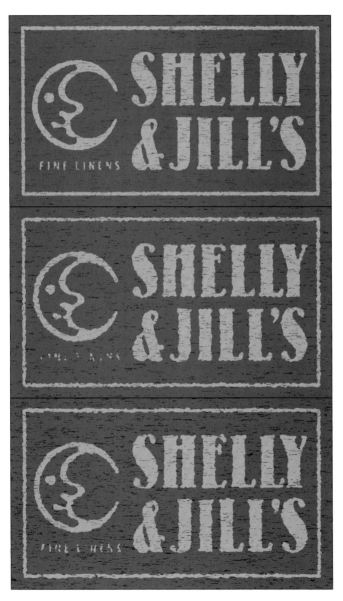

Example 1
Sprayed Strokes:
Stroke Length = 7
Spray Radius = 1

Stamp:
Light/Dark Balance = 7
Smoothness = 3

Example 2
Sprayed Strokes:
Stroke Length = 7
Spray Radius = 7

Stamp:
Light/Dark Balance = 7
Smoothness = 5

Example 3
Sprayed Strokes:
Stroke Length = 10
Spray Radius = 6
Direction = Horizontal

Stamp:
Light/Dark Balance = 7
Smoothness = 4
Mezzotint filter applied twice
on Background Texture and
Extra Texture layers

Create old-fashioned style graphics and type with this technique. First you design the basic graphic or typography in Illustrator. You can design it in Photoshop if you don't have Illustrator, but Illustrator is much easier to use for this part of the technique. Then you'll use Photoshop's filters to roughen up the graphic and apply texture to it and its background. The results are flat, rough, and distressed. It's similar to old woodcut or stenciled graphics.

1. Create a graphic in Illustrator and save it. Open the file in Photoshop. Double-click the layer name in the Layers palette, and rename the layer Graphic.

If you want to create the artwork in Photoshop, use the pen tool, type tool, or shape tools; then choose Layer > Rasterize and select the appropriate layer type.

2. Option/Alt-click the New Layer button in the Layers palette. Name the new layer Background, and fill it with a color. Move the Graphic layer above the Background layer in the Layers palette.

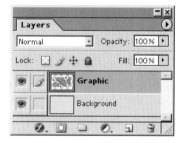

3. Create a selection of the graphic by Command/Ctrl-clicking the thumbnail of the Graphic layer. Choose Select > Save Selection to create a new alpha channel. Name the new channel Graphic. Click OK.

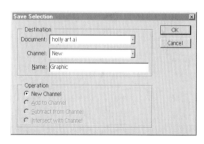

4. Display the Channels palette and click the name "Graphic" to view the Graphic channel. Choose Select > Deselect.

It's necessary to make a channel so that you can use some of the filters in the next steps. The filters give the most consistent results on black-and-white images.

5. Choose Filter > Brush Strokes > Sprayed Strokes. Experiment with the values. The effect will vary depending on the file resolution and the size of the graphics. You want to roughen the edges just a bit in this step. Click OK.

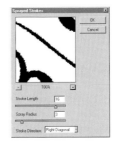

6. Choose Filter > Sketch > Stamp. Experiment with the values. The effect will vary depending on the file resolution and the size of the graphics. This filter will smooth out the edges. Click OK.

7. Return to the Layers palette, and click the Graphic layer to activate it. Option/Alt-click the New Layer button. Create a new layer named Rough Graphic. Turn off the Graphic layer.

8. Choose Select > Load Selection, and choose Graphic as the selection channel. Click OK.

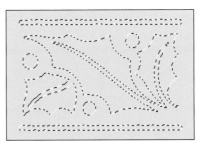

9. Select a foreground color in the Color palette, and press Option + Delete/Alt + Backspace to fill the selection on the Rough Graphic layer. Deselect.

10. Press the D key to return the foreground and background colors to their default values. With the Rough Graphic layer selected in the Layers palette, click the Add Layer Mask button.

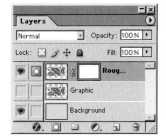

11. Choose Filter > Pixelate > Mezzotint. Select the Medium Strokes type, and click OK.

This will add texture to your graphic. If you want more texture, you can apply the filter more than once.

12. Create a new layer and call it Extra Texture. Repeat steps 8 through 11. Set the layer blending mode to Multiply and adjust the layer Opacity if desired. Click the Extra Texture layer mask and choose Image > Adjustments > Invert. This allows just a small amount of texture to appear on this layer.

13. Create a new layer and call it Background Texture. Repeat steps 9 through 12. Move it just above the Background layer in the Layers palette.

14. If you want to paint parts of your graphic different colors, click the Lock Transparent Pixels button in the Layers palette before you start painting. Don't forget to paint on both the Rough Graphic layer and the Extra Texture layer.

Warhol-style images

Adobe Photoshop 7.0 or later

A prolific painter, Andy Warhol is perhaps best known for his posterized images of soup cans, movie stars, and endangered animals. He used the photographic and printmaking technology available in the '60s and '70s. This technique shows you how to use Photoshop to do what he did. First, open a photograph and use adjustment layers to remove the color and posterize it. You can also selectively burn in or dodge out certain areas of the photo. Once you've prepared the image, you'll add the color. To be true to the Warhol style, use very bright colors. As a final step, you'll add just a few painted highlights to accent certain areas of the image.

1. Open an RGB image. The images that work best with this technique are ones with the subject isolated from the background in some way. If the subject contains similar textures or colors to the background, it will be more difficult to separate the subject from its background in later steps.

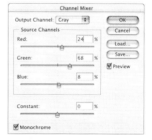

2. Choose Window > Layers to view the Layers palette. Drag the Background layer thumbnail onto the New Layer button at the bottom of the Layers palette to duplicate the layer. It will be named Background Copy.

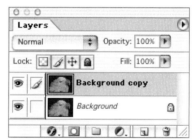

3. Click the New Adjustment Layer button at the bottom of the Layers palette. Choose Channel Mixer from the pop-up menu. Select the Monochrome option, and change the Source Channels to the following values: R = 24, G = 68, B = 8.

Don't worry if your image still needs adjustments— you'll come back to this layer later.

4. Click the New Adjustment Layer button at the bottom of the Layers palette. Select Posterize from the pop-up menu. Make sure that Preview is turned on. Enter a number between 2 and 5. Using a value higher than 5 will make the image look less posterized than Warhol's work. Some of the shapes may blend; you'll fix that in the next few steps.

5. Double-click the Channel Mixer adjustment thumbnail in the Layers palette. Make sure that Preview is turned on. Start making small adjustments to the R, G, and B Source Channel settings to improve the look of your image. Click OK.

In this example, the R and G settings were changed to enlarge the white area around the eye.

6. Select the Background Copy layer in the Layers palette. Select the dodge tool in the toolbox. In the tool options bar, set the Exposure to approximately 15%.

The dodge tool will be used to lighten areas of the image.

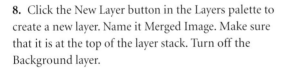

7. Working on the Background Copy layer, use the dodge tool to lighten areas in the image. Use the burn tool (also set to 15% Exposure) to darken areas of the image.

In this example, the lower beak was lightened and the upper beak and lower eye were darkened.

8. Click the New Layer button in the Layers palette to create a new layer. Name it Merged Image. Make sure that it is at the top of the layer stack. Turn off the Background layer.

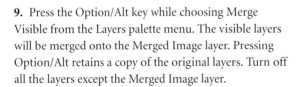

9. Press the Option/Alt key while choosing Merge Visible from the Layers palette menu. The visible layers will be merged onto the Merged Image layer. Pressing Option/Alt retains a copy of the original layers. Turn off all the layers except the Merged Image layer.

Retaining a copy of the other layers is useful if you want to go back and re-edit the image.

10. Select the magic wand tool in the toolbox. In the tool options bar, set the Tolerance to 0; turn off Anti-aliased; turn off Contiguous.

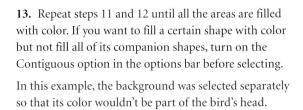

Posterized images have no soft edges, so you don't want the first two options. Contiguous lets you select only one shape at a time. You want to select all of the shapes filled with the same color at a time.

11. Click one area of color in the image to select all shapes painted that color. In this example, all of the black shapes are selected.

12. Select a foreground color in the Color palette. Press Option + Delete/Alt + Backspace to quickly fill a selection with the foreground color. Choose View > Extras to hide the selection edges so that you can evaluate the image. If you are satisfied with the color, continue to the next step. If not, choose another color and refill the selection until you are satisfied.

13. Repeat steps 11 and 12 until all the areas are filled with color. If you want to fill a certain shape with color but not fill all of its companion shapes, turn on the Contiguous option in the options bar before selecting.

In this example, the background was selected separately so that its color wouldn't be part of the bird's head.

14. As a final Warhol touch, make a new layer and add a few contrasting brush strokes to highlight certain parts of the image. If you have a pressure-sensitive tablet and stylus, you'll get the most authentic-looking results.

In this example, the new brush stroke layer was set to the Difference blending mode.

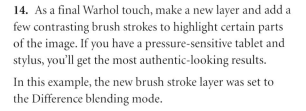

Flat graphics on curved images

Adobe Illustrator 10 or later

Designers frequently have to apply logos, labels, logotypes, or other graphics to photographic images of products, bottles, clothing, and so on. You can add flat graphics to curved shapes in either Photoshop or Illustrator, but Illustrator offers designers more flexibility. Using this technique, you create guides for either cylindrical or spherical forms. Then you use these guides to design an envelope shape that will custom-fit the form to which you are applying the graphic. You then apply the graphic to the envelope. Having the graphic or type in an envelope means you can change it at any time.

1. Open an Illustrator file that contains the logo or graphic to be applied to a curved surface. Create a new layer in the Layers palette, and name it Graphic.

2. Create a new layer in the Layers palette, and name it 3D Image. Move it beneath the Graphic layer.

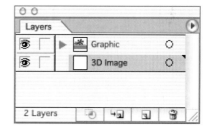

3. With the 3D Image layer still selected, choose File > Place and navigate to the image file to which you will add the graphic. You'll need to add some guides to the image next. For spherical shapes, follow the directions in the technique Making Guides for Spheres. For cylindrical shapes, follow the directions in the technique Making Guides for Cylinders.

Making guides for spheres

1. Hide the Graphic layer in the Layers palette. Move to a different area of the artboard. Select the pen tool in the toolbox. Click the tool once and, holding down the Shift key, click once more a short distance below it to make a vertical line.

2. Click the selection tool in the toolbox; then click the line to select it. Press the Option/Alt key and drag the line to the right. Press the Shift key to constrain the movement. Release the mouse button and then release the Option/Alt and Shift keys to leave a copy behind. Do not deselect.

3. Choose Object > Transform > Transform Again to repeat the transformation. Repeat this command until you have about 5 or 6 lines.

4. Select all of the lines, and double-click the rotate tool in the toolbox. Enter 90° as the angle and click the Copy button to close the dialog box and create a copy.

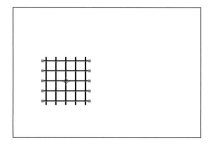

5. Select the ellipse tool in the toolbox, and draw a circle as close to the same size as the circular object in the image.

Press the Shift key to contrain the ellipse to a circle. Press the Option/Alt key to draw from the center point. While drawing the circle, press the spacebar to move the circle around. Release the spacebar to resume drawing.

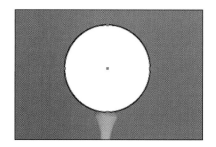

6. Use the selection tool to select both the circle and the grid you completed in step 5.

It's important that the circle be created after the grid because the circle needs to be the frontmost object in the next step.

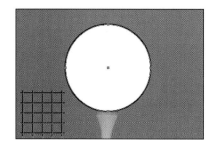

7. Choose Object > Envelope Distort > Make with Top Object.

8. Choose Object > Envelope Distort > Expand. You need to expand the envelope to be able to make guides in the next step.

9. With the sphere lines still selected, choose View > Guides > Make Guides. Now that you have guides, you are ready to finish the graphic distortion technique. Skip to the technique Creating the Curved Envelope.

Making guides for cylinders

1. Hide the Graphic layer in the Layers palette. Select the pen tool in the toolbox. Find the curve at the top of the cylindrical object, and draw a path that imitates it.

2. Deselect the path, and draw a second curve at the bottom of the object. With the selection tool, select both paths.

3. Choose Object > Blend > Make. Then choose Object > Blend > Blend Options. Turn on the Preview option and choose Specified Steps for the Spacing. Try different amounts until you are happy with the spacing. You'll need these lines to make a top and bottom guide for the graphic that you will apply to the cylinder.

4. Choose Object > Blend > Expand to convert the blend into lines.

5. With the lines still selected, choose View > Guides > Make Guides.

6. Use the pen tool to create two lines that directly overlap the left and right edges of the cylindrical object. Select them both.

7. Repeat steps 3 through 5 of this technique to create the vertical guides for the cylinder. Continue with the technique Creating the Curved Envelope.

Creating the curved envelope

1. Select the pen tool in the toolbox. Use the guidelines you created to draw a shape that will contain the graphic or logotype. Make the shape about the size you want the graphic to be.

2. In the Layers palette, show the Graphic layer. The envelope shape should still be selected. Move its selection indicator from the 3D Image layer up onto the Graphic layer.

The envelope shape should be in front of the graphic.

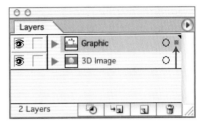

3. Select the envelope shape and the graphic. Don't worry if the graphic isn't the same size as the envelope. Illustrator will fix that in the next step.

4. Choose Object > Envelope Distort > Make with Top Object.

5. Use the direct-selection tool to adjust the envelope, if necessary. Select the envelope, and choose a blending mode in the Transparency palette. This lets the shadows and texture of the photograph show through and makes the graphic look as if it is really printed on the object. The Multiply mode was used in this example. Experiment with modes to see what looks best with your image and graphic.

Appendix A:
Shortcuts and handy tips

Adobe Photoshop 7.0 or later
Adobe Illustrator 10 or later

Frequently used shortcuts for Photoshop		
Shortcut	**Mac OS**	**Windows**
Repeat a task		
Reselect last selection	Shift+Command+D	Shift+Ctrl+D
Use last Levels settings	Option+Command+L	Alt+Ctrl+L
Apply last filter	Command+F	Ctrl+F
Display last filter dialog box	Option+Command+F	Alt+Ctrl+F
Transform with copy	Option+Command+T	Alt+Ctrl+T
Transform again	Shift+Command+T	Shift+Ctrl+T
Transform again with copy	Shift+Command+Option+T	Shift+Alt+Ctrl+T
Moving selected objects		
Leave a copy behind	Option+move tool	Alt+move tool
Constrain movement to 45° or angles set in Preferences	Shift	Shift
Speeding up painting		
Fill with foreground color	Option+Delete	Alt+Backspace
Fill with background color	Command+Delete	Ctrl+Backspace
Get eyedropper while painting	Option	Alt
Select background color (eyedropper)	Option-click a pixel	Alt-click a pixel
Select foreground color (eyedropper)	Click an image pixel	Click an image pixel
Return to default colors	D key	D key
Switch fore- and background colors	X key	X key
Display Fill dialog box	Shift+Delete	Shift+Backspace
Change to smaller brush	[key	[key
Change to larger brush	] key	] key
Paint with straight line (any brush)	Click-Shift-click	Click-Shift-click
Cycle through blend modes	Shift+ – or + keys	Shift+ – or + keys
Set opacity for paint tools	Any number key (e.g., 0 = 100%, 9 = 90%, etc.)	

As stated in the introduction, you should have a basic knowledge of the software and its tools, commands, and palettes before you try the techniques. But because you are busy and overwhelmed and can't always remember all the commands and shortcuts, this appendix contains most of the basic shortcuts that you'll need to efficiently use techniques in this book. Refer to the Quick Reference Card that came in your software box for a complete list of all the keyboard shortcuts.

Frequently used shortcuts for Illustrator		
Shortcut	**Mac OS**	**Windows**
Selecting and transforming		
Last used selection tool	Command key	Ctrl key
Add/subtract from selection	Shift+selection tool	Shift+selection tool
Apply last filter	Command+E	Ctrl+E
Display last filter dialog box	Option+Command+E	Alt+Ctrl+E
Transform again	Shift+Command+T	Shift+Ctrl+T
Set origin point, open dialog box of scale, rotate, shear, or reflect	Option-click with tool	Alt-click with tool
Moving selected objects		
Leave a copy behind	Option+selection tool	Alt+selection tool
Constrain movement to 45° or angles set in Preferences	Shift	Shift
Speeding up painting and drawing		
Copy type's style, color, and size	Select type; click other type with eyedropper	
Constrain proportion for shapes	Shift	Shift
Get smooth tool while painting	Option	Alt
Toggle between eyedropper and paint bucket tools	Option	Alt
Select stroke and fill (eyedropper)	Click a shape	Click a shape
Return to default colors	D key	D key
Switch fill and stroke colors	X key	X key
Select a color from placed image	Shift+eyedropper	Shift+eyedropper
Select a color from gradient	Shift+eyedropper	Shift+eyedropper
Create a tint in Color palette	Shift-drag color slider in Color palette	
Fill/stroke with None	/ key	/ key
Change color to its complement	Command-click color bar	Ctrl-click color bar
Draw with straight line (pen tool)	Click-Shift-click	Click-Shift-click
Change Color palette mode	Shift-click color bar	Shift-click color bar

Frequently used shortcuts for the Layers palette	
Shortcut	**Mac OS/Windows keystrokes**
Both products	
Create and name new layer	Option/Alt-click New Layer button
Delete selected layer	Option/Alt-click Delete/Trash button
Duplicate new layer	Drag layer onto New Layer button
Show/hide just one layer	Option/Alt-click eye column of that layer
Show/hide multiple layers	Drag through eye column
Photoshop	
Disable layer effect temporarily	Click the effect's Show/Hide icon
Make mask on an adjustment layer	Make selection and fill with black
View mask on an adjustment layer	Option/Alt-click adjustment layer thumbnail
View layer mask	Option/Alt-click layer mask thumbnail
Center a layer dragged from another file	Press Shift while dragging layer into window
Combine visible layers onto new layer	Create new layer; Option/Alt+Merge Visible
Create layer mask from selection	Make selection; click Add Layer Mask button
Create layer with a selection	Command/Ctrl+J
Discard/apply a layer mask	Drag layer mask thumbnail to Trash button
Duplicate and name new layer	Option/Alt-drag layer onto New Layer button
Group with the layer below	Command/Ctrl+G
Make/release a clipping group	Option/Alt-click line between layer names
Move several layers at once	Link layers before moving with move tool
Select layer's transparency mask	Command/Ctrl-click layer thumbnail
Turn on/off a layer mask temporarily	Shift-click the layer mask thumbnail
Illustrator	
Copy selection onto a different layer	Option/Alt-drag selection indicator to other layer
Display all but active layer in artwork mode	Command+Option/Ctrl+Alt-click eye icon
Select several contiguous layers	Shift-click layer names
Select several noncontiguous layers	Command/Ctrl-click layer names
Select everything on layer	Option/Alt-click the layer name
Select everything on layer	Click selection indicator area
Toggle preview and artwork mode	Command/Ctrl-click eye column
Unlock all/lock all but one layer	Option/Alt-click lock column of that layer

Frequently used shortcuts for the Layers palette

Photoshop Layers palette

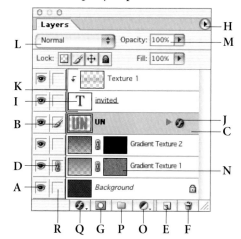

The following letters correspond to the palette images:

A. Shows/hides layer
B. Selected layer
C. Active layer
D. Links/unlinks layer
E. Creates new layer
F. Deletes layer
G. Adds layer mask
H. Displays palette menu
I. Type layer icon
J. Filter effects applied
K. Layer group
L. Layer mode
M. Layer opacity
N. Layer mask
O. Creates new fill or adjustment layer
P. Creates new layer set
Q. Adds layer style
R. Locks/unlocks layer
S. Current selection indicator
T. Creates new sublayer
U. Makes/releases clipping mask
V. Target and appearance indicator

Illustrator Layers palette

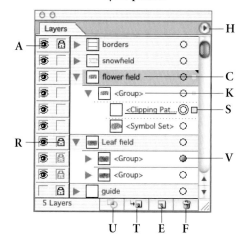

Appendix B: Combining Photoshop and Illustrator files

Adobe Photoshop 7.0 or later
Adobe Illustrator 10 or later

Bringing Photoshop files into Illustrator

There are four different ways to bring Photoshop files into Illustrator: the Place command, drag-and-drop, copy and paste, or the Open command. The drag-and-drop or copy and paste methods are less desirable because the image is converted to a 72-ppi, RGB image. However, you can copy paths created in Photoshop and paste them into an Illustrator file with no loss of image quality. Note, however, that the pasted paths will always be filled and painted with None.

Place command

In Illustrator, choose File > Place and turn on the Link option if you want to link the file; turn off the option if you want to embed the file.

The advantages to linking are that the file size stays small and, although you can't use filters on the linked images, you can update the image using the Links palette.

Open command

In Illustrator, choose File > Open and select the Photoshop image. Illustrator creates an embedded image and enables you to use the Photoshop filters, Photo Cross Hatch filter, or Object Mosaic filters on it. Unfortunately, embedded images become part of the Illustrator file and increase its file size.

Bringing Illustrator artwork into Photoshop

Here's a way to avoid color shift problems when you know you'll be using an Illustrator file in Photoshop: Create the file using RGB colors. If necessary, you can convert the colors to RGB by choosing File > Document Color Mode > RGB Color.

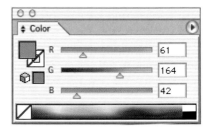

The fact that Photoshop is raster-based and Illustrator is vector-based is important to consider when you're sharing artwork between the two programs. *Raster-based* means that objects are described as pixels on a raster, or grid. As a raster-based program, Photoshop is better for working with organic shapes, such as those in photographs or paintings. *Vector-based* means that objects are mathematically described as points connected by straight or curved lines. Vector-based graphics generated in Illustrator have crisp, clear lines when scaled to any size.

Raster versus vector

Before using Illustrator graphics in Photoshop, evaluate the artwork. Decide whether you want your shapes and type to have sharp, clean edges like the illustration at the right. If so, leave the artwork in Illustrator.

When you open an Illustrator file directly in Photoshop, you'll get the Rasterize dialog box. Minimize stair-stepping on curves by selecting the Anti-alias option. Change the color mode, if desired. Note that Photoshop will rasterize the entire Illustrator file into one image layer if opened this way. To retain the file's layers, export the file from Illustrator (see page 219).

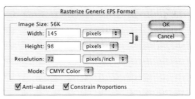

Depending on the file resolution, anti-aliasing can make the edges of objects appear fuzzy. It is generally preferable to the stair-stepping appearance that occurs without it. Note that the thick green line is not improved by anti-aliasing.

On the other hand, if your artwork consists of vertical and horizontal lines and no curves, you can achieve better results without anti-aliasing. In this example, the green line looks sharp, but the curves and angles in the other shapes now have a jagged edge.

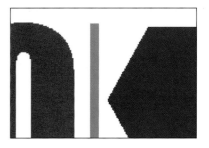

Bringing Illustrator files into Photoshop

As in Photoshop, you can choose from four ways to bring Illustrator files into Photoshop: the Place command, Export and Open, Copy and Paste, or the Open command. If you want to be able to edit layers and text once the Illustrator file is opened in Photoshop, use the Export method. If you want to scale or transform the image to fit with an existing Photoshop file, use the Place method. The Copy and Paste method is best if you want to retain the outlines and use them as paths or shape layers in Photoshop.

Place method

1. In Photoshop, choose File > Place. Navigate to the Illustrator file you want to place, and click Place. Shift-drag the highlighted corners of the box to scale the image proportionally.

The advantage to this method is that you can easily transform the graphic before it is rasterized.

2. When you have finished moving and transforming the graphic, press Return/Enter to complete the rasterization.

Another advantage to placing a graphic is that it is placed on its own layer with a transparent background.

Export method

1. In Illustrator, choose File > Export and select the Photoshop (PSD) format. Be sure to give the file a different name from its Illustrator name. Click Export to open the Photoshop Options dialog box.

2. Select the resolution for the Photoshop file. If you want to keep the layers, choose the Write Layers option. For smooth-edged graphics, choose the Anti-alias option. If your file has text that you want to be able to edit in Photoshop, select the Editable Text option. Click OK.

Being able to edit text is one of the advantages of using this method.

3. Open the file in Photoshop.

The disadvantage to this method is that the file will be exactly the size of the graphics and no larger. If you want to add space around the edges of the graphic, choose Image > Canvas Size and increase the size of the canvas.

Copy and Paste

1. Before copying the Illustrator graphic, choose Illustrator > Preferences > Files & Clipboard (Mac OS X) or Edit > Preferences > Files & Clipboard (Mac OS/ Windows). To retain the paths in the file, select the AICB option, and choose Preserve Paths. Click OK. Choose Edit > Copy to copy the selected artwork.

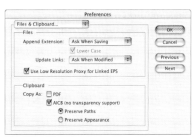

2. In Photoshop, choose Edit > Paste. Choose one of the three options in the Paste dialog box. Click OK to paste the graphic.

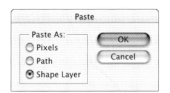

3. Note that choosing the Shape Layer option fills the graphic with the current foreground color. If you chose Pixels, the graphic is filled with the color specified in Illustrator; to transform it before rasterizing, press Return/Enter. If you chose Shape Layer, as in this example, the size is the exact size it was in Illustrator; to change it, choose Edit > Free Transform.

Open method

Choose File > Open and open the Illustrator file. Choose the size, mode, and resolution, and click OK.

The file will open with all layers merged onto one layer. Be sure to rename the file when saving so as not to overwrite the original Illustrator file.

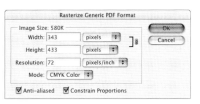

Recommended Reading

ADOBE DEVELOPMENT TEAM. *Adobe Illustrator 10 Classroom in a Book* (The Classroom in a Book Series). San Jose, CA: Adobe Press, 2002.

———. *Adobe Photoshop 7 Classroom in a Book*. San Jose, CA: Adobe Press, 2002.

———. *Adobe Photoshop 6.0 and Adobe Illustrator 9.0 Advanced Classroom in a Book*. San Jose, CA: Adobe Press, 2001.

ALSPACH, TED, PIERRE E. BÉZIER, AND KELLY L. MURDOCK. *Illustrator 10 Bible*. Hungry Minds, Inc., 2002.

BIEDNY, DAVID, BERT MONROY, AND NATHAN MOODY. *Photoshop Channel Chops*. Indianapolis, IN: New Riders Publishing, 1998.

BLATNER, DAVID, AND BRUCE FRASER. *Real World Photoshop 7* (Real World Series). Berkeley, CA: Peachpit Press, 2002.

CAMERON, JULIA. *The Artist's Way.* New York, NY: Tarcher/Putnam, 1992.

DAYTON, LINNEA, AND JACK DAVIS. *The Photoshop 7 Wow! Book*. Berkeley, CA: Peachpit Press, 2002.

EISMANN, KATRIN. *Photoshop Restoration & Retouching*. Indianapolis, IN: Que Publishing, 2001.

FRASER, BRUCE , FRED BUNTING, AND CHRIS MURPHY. *Real World Color Management* (Real World Series). Berkeley, CA: Peachpit Press, 2002.

HAYNES, BARRY. *Photoshop 7 Artistry*. Indianapolis, IN: New Riders Publishing, 2002.

LONDON, SHERRY, AND RHODA GROSSMAN. *Photoshop 7 Magic*. Indianapolis, IN: New Riders Publishing, 2002.

MCCLELLAND, DEKE. *Adobe Master Class: Design Invitational*. Berkeley, CA: Peachpit Press, 2002.

———. *MacWorld Photoshop 6 Bible*. Hungry Minds, Inc. 2000.

———. *Real World Illustrator 10*. Berkeley, CA: Peachpit Press, 2002.

———. *Real World Digital Photography*. Berkeley, CA: Peachpit Press, 1999.

———. *Photoshop Studio Secrets (Secrets)*. Hungry Minds, Inc., 2001.

MCCLOUD, SCOTT. *Understanding Comics*. New York, NY: HarperCollins, 1993.

MONROY, BERT. *Bert Monroy: Photorealistic Techniques with Photoshop & Illustrator*. Indianapolis, IN: New Riders Publishing, 2000.

PFIFFNER, PAMELA. *Inside the Publishing Revolution: The Adobe Story*. Berkeley, CA: Peachpit Press, 2002.

SIEGEL, DAVID. *Creating Killer Web Sites, Second Edition*. Indianapolis, IN: Hayden Books, 1997.

STEUER, SHARON. *The Illustrator 10 Wow! Book*. Berkeley, CA: Peachpit Press, 2002.

TUFTE, EDWARD R. *The Visual Display of Quantitative Information*. Cheshire, CT: Graphics Press, 1983.

WEINMAN, LYNDA. *Designing Web Graphics 3*. Indianapolis, IN: New Riders Publishing, 1999.

WEINMAN, LYNDA, AND JAN KABILI. *Photoshop 6 ImageReady 3 Hands-on Training*. Berkeley, CA: Peachpit Press, 2001.

WEINMANN, ELAINE, AND PETER LOUREKAS. *Illustrator 10 for Windows and Macintosh* (Visual Quickstart Guide Series). Berkeley, CA: Peachpit Press, 2002.
———. *Photoshop 7 for Windows and Macintosh: Visual QuickStart Guide.* Berkeley, CA: Peachpit Press, 2002.

WILLIAMS, ROBIN, JOHN TOLLETT, AND DAVID ROHR. *Robin Williams Web Design Workshop.* Berkeley, CA: Peachpit Press, 2001.

WILLMORE, BEN. *Adobe Photoshop 7.0 Studio Techniques.* Indianapolis, IN: Adobe Press, 2002.

Index

Credits

Author:	Luanne Seymour Cohen
Book Design/Production:	Jan Martí
Cover Design:	Michael Mabry
Executive Editor:	Becky Morgan
Copy Editor:	Judy Walthers von Alten
Indexer:	Judy Walthers von Alten
Testers:	Carol Bly
	Kaoru Hollin

Photography and illustration credits

All photography and illustration were done by Luanne Seymour Cohen unless noted in the chart below. Italics indicate large focal illustrations.

Photographer/Artist	Page number(s)
Artbeats	63 (wood)
Classic PIO Library	93 (fabric)
Kaoru Hollin	*48, 90, 98*
Aren K. Howell	*92*
Illustrator 8 CD Brush Library	48 (box)
Michael Mabry	*86 (illus. from Design Essentials, 3rd Edition cover)*
Kathi Fox	216
PhotoDisc	8, 31, 45, 86 *(photo)*, 112, 116, 120, *154 (texture)*, *166, 174-5, 187-8, 202*, 203, *206 (photo)*, 207, 209
Ultimate Symbol, Inc.	*132, 198 (moon)*, 199, *214*
Unknown	38 (woman)

Colophon

This book was designed and produced using Adobe PageMaker 6.5, Adobe Illustrator 10, and Adobe Photoshop 7.0. The Adobe Original Minion and Minion Expert typefaces are used throughout the book.